# *Endorsement*

"I've known the author for decades and have had the pleasure of working with her in numerous Army assignments. Irene's book is funny, candid, informative and poignant; I'm certain it will inspire soldiers, particularly women, as they blaze their own exciting paths in uniform."

—Kate Leahy, Major General (Retired), U.S. Army

# CHOOSE YOUR BATTLES

ONE WOMAN'S INSPIRING JOURNEY THROUGH THE RANKS

**IRENE VAISHVILA GLAESER**
(COL. U.S. ARMY RETIRED)

Copyright © 2023 by Irene V. Glaeser
First Paperback Edition

All rights reserved. No part of this publication may be reproduced, distributed, or transmitted in any form or by any means, including photocopying, recording, or other electronic or mechanical methods, without the prior written permission of the publisher, except in the case of brief quotations embodied in critical reviews and certain other noncommercial uses permitted by copyright law. For permission requests, write to the publisher, addressed "Attention: Permissions Coordinator," at the address below.

Some names, businesses, places, events, locales, incidents, and identifying details inside this book have been changed to protect the privacy of individuals.

Published by Freiling Agency, LLC.

P.O. Box 1264
Warrenton, VA 20188

www.FreilingAgency.com

PB ISBN: 979-8-9881634-4-2
eBook ISBN: 979-8-9881634-5-9

*Printed in the United States of America*

# Table of Contents

Introduction ........................................................ vii
1   Synergy ........................................................ 1
2   Stand ............................................................ 13
3   Trends .......................................................... 21
4   Hydrate ........................................................ 31
5   Guilt ............................................................. 41
6   Training ....................................................... 51
7   Shine ............................................................ 61
8   Landings ...................................................... 71
9   Choose ......................................................... 79
10   Modesty ..................................................... 87
11   Repeat ........................................................ 97
12   Cheer .......................................................... 107
13   Camaraderie ............................................. 117

If you dare to jump,

you can soar.

# INTRODUCTION

## *Soar*

Formal integration of women into the armed forces was a slow and gradual process in spite of the history of heroic women serving in wars. The Women's Army Corps was formed in 1942 and later disbanded in 1978, ending all-female units. Women were accepted into the service academies in 1976. In 1983 I decided to join the Army at a time when nearly all combat arms specialties were still closed to women. It would be a decade longer before full integration of women into those jobs. My unit would send me to the Army Airborne School at Fort Benning, Georgia, otherwise known as Jump School. Women were first allowed there in 1976, but there were very few of us at the time.

The thought of parachuting from an airplane (or helicopter, as I did later) isn't easily described. There's no sudden drop or endless pit in your stomach—it's loud, intense, windy, and completely exhilarating. An initial wall of resistance meets your leap from the plane before you relax into a cloud of cushioning air currents that carry you downward through the sky. At first, it feels like a vortex of loud wind and aircraft noise before the chute deploys and euphoria kicks in—finally, relaxation and the incredible sensation of being supported by the air beneath you. Instead of falling, you are flying for that short period of time before the ground comes up, and you have to get busy to land properly and execute all the next steps you've trained so hard to learn.

In 1983, the same year that President Ronald Reagan called the Soviet Union "the evil empire," I was a newly minted private first class, having some rank after my one-year college transcripts came through. Women were beginning to join the ranks of the Army in more significant numbers. Why wouldn't we, with a catchy recruiting tune of "BE, all that you can BE!" running through our collective conscience? However, more than nine out of every ten soldiers were male. It was not until 2015 that most combat arms positions would open to women. So, I suppose you could say I was a pioneer, as were my handful of female peers that summer, but we didn't realize that, nor did we own it. I just wanted to make it through jump school! We females experienced things differently, and the obstacles and challenges were around each corner, invisible to our male counterparts. Always restless, I found the Army held enormous appeal to me. I signed up for the military

## Introduction

experience and was eager to take unknown risks to be trained and ready to serve our great Nation.

At least 550 trainees in the form of officers, noncommissioned officers, junior enlisted, and cadets arrived and checked into Fort Benning, Georgia, in August of 1983. Those of us junior enlisted (almost all were male) experienced a week of in-processing, medical and fitness tests, and mindless tasks during what was called Zero Week. The heat and humidity felt like a daily sauna turned up a little too high. Fort Dix, New Jersey, where I had my basic training, had nothing on Fort Benning. As the males were sent in those broiling temperatures to cut grass and "spitshine" (only a term of art) the company area, I was brought inside to type and file. I remember staring out the window and feeling more than a little annoyed that I was not tasked to cut grass. First of all, I would make pocket change as a young girl cutting my parents' grass with a hand mower, and second, there is nothing in the world like the smell of fresh-cut grass. And I love the heat. I always have. I didn't like starting out my training being segregated from the males I would be training with for the following three weeks.

That week we were issued all of our gear. We each received a helmet, with a letter and/or number taped on the front, indicating our status when we arrived.

Officers, noncommissioned officers, and cadets were all identified by a letter. However, junior enlisted received a number without an identifying letter. For everyone but me, the numbers began at one hundred and went upward from there. It took me a while to realize that my issued number eleven was set apart. There was no one to ten, and there was no twelve to ninety-nine. Yet somehow, mine was number eleven. Why eleven? My number stood out from all the rest. As if I didn't already stand out? OK, I thought. I will play that game and take on whatever it meant, and I was to learn fairly quickly.

Beginning the first week, the first sergeant called all of us into a very large formation several times a day. He then barked out groups he chose to single out: ALL LEG RANGERS (non-Airborne) Rangers, DO PUSHUPS!!!, Navy SEALS, Marines, and Air Force were next. At the end of the line was me, "Number Eleven." Suddenly, the first sergeant's voice altered into a high-pitched imitation of a girlish falsetto as he smirked and said softly but loud enough for everyone to hear, "Number Eleven, Do push-ups!" I could hear others quietly laughing in the background as I fell into a front-leaning rest position (pushup position) while barking out my enthusiasm in a distinctly non-female-sounding voice. Unlike the first sergeant's more feminine falsetto, my voice has a gravelly tenor that sounds far from girly, due to

## Introduction

vocal cord damage and surgery. That first sergeant, whose name and face I will never forget, actually did me a favor. He made me want to work harder. I loved Army training, and I loved doing push-ups. When I finally experienced jumping, it knocked me back at first. But adapting to the subsequent rush was exhilarating, and heck, no one there doubted that I could do pushups.

Training continued that hot, dusty summer at Fort Benning. I kept on training and watched as trainees dropped out with injuries and even fear. I was not going to give up. We junior enlisted had no time off, and after training at night, we had various tasks to perform. With our early mornings and the constant heat, sometimes staying awake became a challenge. Falling asleep during the "classroom" (read, bleachers) portion of the training was not uncommon, and cadre members (called blackhats for their black berets) would patrol and find the errant sleepers. Once, during swing landing training, a more than critical portion of the training, I dozed off. Calamity!

"Number Eleven!! Beat your boots!!" (Darn that easily remembered number!) I had to stand up and off to the side of the bleachers in plain sight of every trainee and beat my boots. This involved standing erect and bending my knees while slapping the sides of my boots, maintaining perfect posture, at least one hundred times. It was embarrassing and somewhat comical in appearance, but something about the camaraderie I had started to experience kicked in, and I did not let it get me down. The coveted Airborne wings were well worth it. As more and more trainees fell out, I felt like I was starting to stand out in a different way—earning grudging respect as I passed through training gates. At one point, I learned from a cadre member that there had been a bet going that I would not survive.

Attitude is everything, and shared experiences further connected me to my enlisted peers. There were twelve of us in a "chalk," and I was, of course, the only female. My previous training had been with all women, but I learned to deal with and, yes, thrive in this integrated environment. Times were very different, and we stood in lines to drop coins in the handful of phone booths when we were allowed. We called mothers, spouses, children, boyfriends, and girlfriends until the annoyed line behind us informed us we were done. We all came from different backgrounds and cultures; training was our common denominator as we negotiated obstacles together. An amusing obstacle was evidenced in the mess hall. This was a colloquial term for the dining facility. Our mess hall only had room for about half of the initial cohort of trainees. We had to consume, wolf-down being the reality, our food as fast as we could because blackhats would stroll through the mess hall and tap us on the shoulder, saying quietly with a gleam in their eyes, "You're done; get up" — one run-on sentence. This would even occur as we took our first bite. I could eat quickly and laughed when I saw trainees running out of the mess hall with half a hamburger sticking out of their mouths and bananas sticking out of their side pockets. Jump school was not one for delicate stomachs as we went from eating to resuming running to all our training locations.

Training was all grueling hard work in temperatures that felt like 115 degrees in the Georgia humidity. It didn't take long for the 550 to whittle down to 500, 400, and so on. Daily injuries due to accidents and inattention to the instructions reduced our numbers. Tower week involved raising us individually up a thirty-four-foot tower (still the icons visible at Fort Benning today) and dropping us to test our ability to conduct a four-point landing, the fourth point of contact being our buttocks. Get your head out of your fourth point of contact!! —This was an often-heard admonishment yelled at very high decibels. Every day there would be a few more trainees on crutches, a gloomy beginning to our process. Those of us remaining grew in confidence and anticipation. Still, fearing injuries, there was always this little knot in my stomach.

What kept me going? I had this pattern of committing first and being nervous as an afterthought. I remember, as a twelve-year-old girl, going up in a WWII biplane at the Bealeton Flying Circus in Warrenton, Virginia. That tiny plane did loop-di-loops with just me and the pilot in it! I recalled the rush it gave me. Airborne training was excellent (the school had been around since WWII) and prepared me well for the penultimate moment when my turn arrived to make my first jump. I had signed up for this, I had trained for this, and I was ready for the big day.

*This is it. I could die,* I remember thinking. We finally boarded the C-130 aircraft on that pivotal day after sitting on the broiling tarmac in all our gear for what felt like centuries. We ascended, and we were all silent, lost in our own thoughts. I mentally reviewed the steps I had learned to myself. The jumpmaster turned and held up six digits— a full hand and an index finger. "SIX MINUTES," he barked. I gulped. We had all been taught a proper exit involving counting, "One thousand. Two thousand. Three thousand. Four thousand." The chute would deploy in a rush that would yank us upward, and then we would be soaring. I visualized each

## Introduction

count and each movement I would take as I took deep breaths to calm my racing heart.

When I jumped, it was on a gasp of a prayer. All my Lutheran catechism rushed back to me. I looked to God to help me negotiate this first jump. "Our Father (one thousand), who art in Heaven (two thousand), hallowed be thy Name (three thousand)" ...*whoosh!* The chute deployed as I spoke the word *Name*, abruptly ending my recitation of The Lord's Prayer. I thanked God and looked briefly at the heavens before drifting downward. I was sure that The Lord's Prayer had kept me safe.

I'm sometimes asked about those early days in the Army of the 80s and about everything that's happened since then as a female soldier. Years later, as Colonel Irene Glaeser, I've had the honor of serving next to some of America's finest, from privates to general officers, men and women who love service. From a nervous young enlisted soldier to a commissioned military police officer and inspector general, and later as a federal government official, I had come a long way since 1983.

Today, women are breaking barriers everywhere in the military, serving in combat, on ships and submarines, and as combat pilots, achieving things that were not yet heard of in 1983. Sometimes young women ask me how I did it and what advice I can give them.

"Work hard, be kind, pray more, tell the truth, and be proud to stand out," I reply. "Pick your battles."

This book is my story about how I learned to practice those words. It is a list of life lessons I have learned throughout my experience in the Army and beyond. Your path won't be the same as the one I chose. Still, you may find you appreciate my challenges as they paralleled challenges you have had in your own life journey. When we women step into our strengths and abilities and learn from others, we can achieve things that earlier generations never thought possible.

Leverage your strength by shining your teammate's boots...and vice versa.

# 1

# *Synergy*

In May of 1983, I arrived at Fort Dix, New Jersey, to join my all-female Army basic training company. Only five years had passed since the Women's Army Corps disbanded, and female recruits still trained separately from the males. I was nervous and anxious but very excited. I was facing the unknown. My father had served, as well as my older sister, so I had the advantage of a female role model. I had briefly considered the Marine Corps but knew that the Army had significant numbers in Germany back then. With a German mother, I was motivated to see the world, beginning with Germany. Assignments were not guaranteed by any means, but I knew what I wanted. The Army appealed to me the most because I loved running and shooting and did both in high school. Most of all, I wanted to serve.

Alpha Company was followed in line by exclusively male companies Bravo through Delta. We looked different, and we sounded different because we *were* different. Our cadences had a higher and softer pitch, excluding me as my tenor-sounding timbre had often caused me to be mistaken for a boy on the phone. Our differences didn't intimidate us—they inspired us to be better, prepare harder, and break past invisible boundaries set by a male-dominated domain. In a rare moment of non-screaming candor, our male drill sergeant told us that his female recruits worked harder, and he preferred to train them. We didn't arrive with chips on our shoulders; we were carrying the weight of a legacy that future women could follow, and we were building that trail for them.

Upon our arrival at Fort Dix, buses, looking a lot like repurposed school buses, transported us around to various in-processing stations as we filled out miles of paperwork. "Always use a black pen!" "Don't use a boyfriend as a beneficiary!" "Your home of record is your point of entry to the Army!" "I did not tell you to fill out the next block!!" We went to a central issue facility, or CIF, and received our issue items; they filled two duffel bags. I gasped at the hideous seafoam-colored green blouse and shirt with gold buttons when they were handed to me. They gleamed in their polyester, about-to-be-phased-out glory. We surrendered the clothing that we arrived in and were given a class on how to wear the uniform. Our individuality was homogenized as we blended together in a sea of brand-new camouflage uniforms. Until recently, soldiers wore plain olive drab field uniforms with white T-shirts. In garrison, or basically while not conducting field training, these uniforms were crisply pressed and worn with a small black web belt whose buckle perfectly aligned with the blouse buttons and pants zipper —a "gig line." The camouflage pattern was new and came with a brown T-shirt. Pressing was still a requirement, but the effect was far less noticeable.

The daughter of two naturalized immigrants, my German and Lithuanian ancestry (fair) was on full display when we wore those seafoam-colored plastic dress uniforms. My skin turned the verdant tone of seasickness as my pale skin reflected a ghoulish green-slime-like glow. I also received a gorgeous mini-balloon of a black round felt dress hat. We all referred to those as our mushroom caps, and believe me, they looked ridiculous. Finally, I surrendered my contact lenses and was handed black glasses along with my myopic peers. The frames, so nerdy at the time and so trendy much later, were unlovingly referred to as "RPGs"- rape prevention glasses; or "BCGs," birth control glasses. I was grateful that we trained then without males present because the glasses made me feel self-conscious. I was doubly grateful we spent almost all our time in camouflage versus the seafoam!

My nametag read "Vaishvila." To me, it was a badge of honor representing my father's country, little-known at that time before the internet. The Lithuanian people were warriors whose country was occupied by Russia during that Cold War period. My father could not return. They fiercely struggled under the weight of that occupation and were not even allowed to practice their predominantly Catholic faith. Lithuania is a very strong ally today, and the U.S. sends troops to train there should the now-struggling Russian war machine approach it. My name had no meaning to the drill sergeants, who immediately resorted to calling me "Vice Versa." Drill sergeants gave such names to anyone with unpronounceable last names. Interestingly in 1983, there were very few ethnic-sounding names to wrestle with, something completely opposite today. I would be stuck with Vice Versa for the entire training cycle.

I hated this moniker. It hounded me daily: "Vice Versa, drop and do push-ups!" "Vice Versa, move out!" "Vice Versa, you are on KP duty today!" (KP basically meant cleaning our mess hall). It grated on my nerves to hear the constant butchering of my name, but honestly, I pretty much had it butchered by teachers in grade school all my life already. Roll call sounded like this: (Teacher) "V-V-V-V-" (Me) "HERE!"

We were constantly being yelled at and always on the go. We did physical fitness exercises, ran through gas chambers, took classes, practiced on firing ranges, trained in the field, and shoveled food into our faces in our limited time in the mess halls. Thinking about that summer reminds me of exhaustion, brutal heat, hair-raising humidity, and sand in all possible cracks and crevices of my body. I worked very hard not to be the target of the drill sergeant's ire, and for the most part, I wasn't. My track, cross country, and rifle team background served me very well in basic training.

Army training was a grit-filled fight for gains. My company was made up of primarily young females, but I do not remember training with any mothers. Seventeen-year-old minor females needed their parents' consent to enlist, a practice still in effect today. Our days were filled, leaving no time to become acquainted. However, later in the day and in the evenings, we often had some time to prepare our gear for the next day. Then, the simple act of boot polishing brought us together because we could speak freely and share our thoughts.

Housed in old World War II Army barracks, we were assigned the bunks lining the room in a precise symmetrical pattern. When we were issued our boots, they came with a class on how to shine them until they gleamed in a glassy obsidian glow. This involved a moist rag and moisture; read: spit. Therefore, the term spitshine applied. The glassier the boot, the more squared away the recruit, and mastering this task was critical to success.

Just as with grass cutting, I had received pocket change for shining the military shoes my father wore daily to the Pentagon. Unlike many other female recruits that summer, I had shined shoes for years and found in the task a sense of calm and satisfaction. Using a rag, boot black, spit, and a circular and repetitive motion, the result was a clearing of my mind, similar to how a windshield wiper clears water. It was a mindless exercise, my hands repeating the pattern over the surface of the boots emphasizing the toes, the inky black polish stinging my nostrils with a familiar pungent scent.

This activity occurred in the evenings. We gathered and sat on the stoops of the barracks and polished our boots. Some of us talked and traded stories about ourselves. The bonding would sometimes keep us there longer than the time it took to finish the task, and we forged friendships in those moments.

Our barracks floor had two small rooms at the entrance. I noticed these on the first day as we received our walk-through and instructions. One held a lone bunk, while the other room was appointed with two bunks. My drill sergeant informed us that the room with the two bunks belonged to the company and platoon guidon (flag) bearers because, as Alpha company, we marched first. The company guidon bearer would march in front of the entire company. She had already been selected. They had not chosen the platoon guidon bearer. As much as I loved the camaraderie of the other women, having a little privacy in that space for those six weeks was a very enticing idea.

"If you want to be the guidon bearer, you will have to carry the guidon wherever you go. You will sleep with it. You will eat with it. You will watch it while you shower. Consider it your new boyfriend," our drill sergeant barked.

"I'm in!" My hand shot up. Others had shirked additional responsibility, but I had already gazed upon my new boyfriend with stars in my eyes. My new boyfriend and I were to have a semi-private room all summer— I was instantly in love! I was always a light sleeper, easily startled by sounds. Okay... high strung; I will admit that. I wanted my short-allotted sleep cycles to count! I was unceremoniously presented with the deep crimson guidon that was to become my constant companion. I would cherish it and guard it with my life, as drill sergeants were wont to snatch it in a weak moment of vigilance.

This never happened to me! My guidon reposed next to me in my bunk and the field. I never regretted this decision and loved the added privacy at night.

I shared the room with a young private from Harlem, New York. She did not bother trying to pronounce my last name, but we quickly became fast friends during that training cycle.

"Vice Versa," my roommate called early in our new-found relationship at the boot-shining stoop. "You do my boots for me." It was not a question.

"Uh, ok…and why would I want to do that?" I returned to my regular boot polishing ritual.

Pensive for a moment, she replied, "I'll iron your uniforms for you." We didn't have to starch our field uniforms, but they couldn't look like a wrinkle bomb went off either. Our dress blouses, skirts, and trousers had to be ironed to a snappy sharpness that seemed almost unobtainable. While I was out polishing boots and cutting grass growing up, indoor cleaning and ironing were entirely unappealing for me. My mother would kick me out of the house and smooth our clothes and, yes, pillowcases and my father's handkerchiefs to perfection. I believe my mother enjoyed the ritual and her alone time, and I never interfered with it.

# Synergy

"Deal!" I replied to my roommate. We all need a little Zen, particularly after a day of being screamed at hoarsely by drill sergeants, often irritated by lack of sleep and our proven (in the early days) stupidity. I was pretty sure that no one could iron like my mother, but if it gave my roommate the Zen-like peace I witnessed at home with the result of a crisp uniform, I realized I got the better end of the deal. I was so happy she offered. It seemed a fair trade.

My roommate and I quietly exchanged tasks that benefited each other. We kept it under the radar, but it improved our morale and eased the harsh burden of responsibility by using our strengths instead of working on our weaknesses. We kept our room immaculately clean. We both made our beds with hospital corners wrapped so tightly you could bounce a quarter off them, which was the goal. We swept up dust, debris, and tiny bugs so our room would pass the strictest scrutiny, and we learned a valuable lesson. We became stronger by covering for each other's weaknesses.

I hated losing touch after basic training, but we did not have computers, Facebook, or smartphones back then. We could only reconnect if we bumped into each other in Post Exchanges around the world or assignments together. I lost track of my roommate, but I will never forget her.

Shared strengths produce a synergy of effort. I learned early to build teams and surround myself with others whose abilities would strengthen my weaknesses. This allowed me to improve not only those weaknesses but also my strengths. None of us are an island, and spending too much effort on weaknesses will only inhibit growth. Learn from others.

When you stand out,

consider it a privilege.

# 2

## *Stand*

"Viiiice- versssssssssssa!!" The usual butchering of my name assaulted my sensibilities yet again. The young private first class tasked to support cadet training that summer spewed out my last name like some sort of nightmare alphabet soup.

"Vish Vish? What the hell is that?" he barked.

"It's Lithuanian," I replied, sighing heavily.

"Lithuania? Where on earth is THAT?" he demanded hoarsely in loud decibels.

"It's above Poland."

"Is that behind the Iron Curtain?" he persisted relentlessly.

"Yes, it is," I replied, used to this line of questioning.

"So, you must be a COMMUNIST," he stated triumphantly. He had a new victim to torment, and victims were fun! "You are a communist," he said, pointing this time and raising his voice as he grew more confident in his assertion. "Communist!"

It was the summer of 1984, and I was at Fort Bragg, N.C., for Army Reserve Officer Training Corps (ROTC) Advanced Camp. That was what it was known as back then. It is now referred to as LDAC, the acronym for the "Leader Development and Assessment Course." The Camp moniker went out the wayside as it sounded like a fun summer at Boy or Girl Scout camp, and Scout Camp it most assuredly was not. Officer candidates (cadets), assembled from colleges and universities up and down the eastern seaboard, were put through rigorous paces to assess their leadership potential. The training was the great equalizer, blending students from various walks of life: those who had immigrated and were seeking U.S. Citizenship, to those who had grown up on farms, inner cities, or suburbs. The pressure was constant as our every move was continuously monitored by both assigned and peer cadet cadre for nascent leadership qualities. (*Cadet Snuffy exhibited flawed judgment by allowing his platoon to snack while completing training*). These assessors were omnipresent with their notebooks and stubby pencils, hovering in plain or concealed sight, sealing our fates over one bad move. The competition was fierce but also friendly —we were all in this together—as we clambered to excel and rise above the others in the race for a top position on the Order of Merit List, a military version of the Holy Grail. A high number gave us better odds of being selected for our coveted branch of the Army (there were eighteen back then) and, if we were very lucky, the duty assignment location of our dreams. This did not happen in many cases, but hope filled our hearts in the summer of 1984.

Today, LDAC is a very intensely rigorous program. It was in my day as well; it certainly had its moments. We were given time off on most weekends when we could don our civilian clothes and decompress at the Fort Benning Officer's Club, among others, which helped us blow off steam. That's when I became abundantly aware of how few women really were in that training.

Following Vietnam, the first conflict the Army entered into was Grenada in 1983. This island invasion was to rescue and extract all U.S. Citizens, primarily medical students, from the civil strife which had become dangerous. Troops from the 82nd Airborne Division at Fort Bragg, 75th Ranger Regiment, Delta Force, and Marines were involved. Shots were fired, and Combat Infantry Badges were later awarded to the Army troops serving there. As a result, many young soldiers from the 82nd bore the badges and did so proudly as they relished the free reign they held to shout at cadets (no obscenities, please). One event, the "Slide for Life," was a perfect opportunity to taunt me for my heritage— I was not the only one, but my last name made me stick out.

The Slide for Life was a rough rope suspended approximately thirty feet in the air that cadets slid down on a pulley of sorts until they were told to let go and go hurling, uniform and all, into the water. It seemed to be some sort of zipline experience, and I eagerly anticipated the adventure. The fun evaporated quickly. Those who struggled with a fear of heights or water found it a daunting terror-filled foe. I wasn't fazed as I stood in line, awaiting my turn. This challenge was an equalizer; males and females could succeed or fail in equal measure. I knew that I would master it.

I did not predict that I would do so while mirthful echoes of "Communist!" could be heard clearly across the water. With no chance of unobtrusively blending in, I was now tasked with making my way across the line while shouting at the top of my lungs, "I love my country! I love my country! I love my country!"

Achievement accomplished, albeit with taint on the tarnished triumph. As the summer progressed, my efforts to prove myself among my mostly male peers would continue, often in vain.

We spent water survival training day in the pool, where we swam 100 meters for speed, twenty-five meters in uniform, and learned how to inflate our uniforms and make flotation devices out of them. It was a very tough day for anyone who was not a strong swimmer, but I had been a lifeguard all through high school. I was confident in my swimming skills and couldn't wait to cool off in the pool that hot, humid summer. I really looked forward to this part of the training.

Female cadets weren't issued swimsuits. Instead, we were issued instructions. We were told to bring a solid-colored one-piece suit. I chose a conservative black swimsuit, grateful for my not-curvy figure.

Despite my plans, it soon became evident that blending in was again a goal I would not accomplish that day. Most squads had one female assigned, meaning there were perhaps four or five women in an entire platoon. I was one of these. The females were all housed separately from the males, yet we trained with the men from sunup to sundown. We secretly sought to maintain the highest level of performance without drawing unnecessary attention to ourselves due to the separateness of our living arrangements. It was difficult. There were times we were not informed of last-minute changes to our orders, and sometimes we suspected it was by design. Huffing and puffing, due to the distance of the female barracks, the four of us would forge our way to the formation when we received the word, sliding late into formation amid snickers.

The night before water survival day, I discovered I would be the company first sergeant the next day. Leadership roles rotated daily and sometimes more often ("you are DEAD, next one in place!"). We were assessed and evaluated on how well we planned and organized based on our place in the chain of command or pecking order. To be a cadet first sergeant carried a lot of responsibility for the safety and welfare of all the cadets, so it was an assignment that I took seriously. There were training missions but also real-world missions of ensuring the canteens were full and everyone drank to combat the effects of the blistering sun. First sergeant was a position I had never intended to carry out dressed in a swimsuit and flip-flops.

The following day after receiving my orders, I ran out dressed in my uniform of the day, which happened to be a bathing suit, as the company "fell in" to formation, standing at attention in ranks in front of me. I proceeded to issue commands while trying not to feel ridiculous. I could practically feel a cadre member breathing down the back of my neck after becoming aware of the reality of the situation, warding off any possible inappropriate remarks. All I could think of was, *Really? Couldn't they give just this day to a male???* I still laugh when I think about it.

I spoke with authority and stood erect while commanding the company to "Forward, March" towards our training location, flip-flops flapping in the dust. The day went well for me. Most importantly, no one was hurt. I figured that if I could confidently lead in flip-flops, I could lead well anywhere. If my assignment as First Sergeant that particular day was designed to embarrass me, it had the opposite effect. I learned that leadership is created in character and not based on clothing or appearance.

Thankfully, appearance didn't equal authority because that would not be the last time I drew unwanted attention to myself. My experience at Advanced Camp that summer taught me that whether it was due to my immigrant last name or being one of only a handful of females in my company, I could not help but stand out. I learned that if I had no choice but to stand out, it was critical to do it to the best of my abilities. I wanted to stand out for the right reasons and not superficial ones.

Trends pass—

follow your heart

and blaze new trails.

# 3

## *Trends*

In 1988, I found myself in an airplane hangar somewhere in the northern part of divided West Germany. We were there to provide customs support to the high-ranking U.S. officials there to view training, associated with the enormous Return of Forces to Germany (REFORGER) exercise. At that time, there was a NATO agreement that allowed Soviet bloc countries to view the training as well. High-ranking officers, wearing hammer and sickle insignia within a star on their headgear, entered that hangar, led by an assertive captain who was a liaison officer from the White House. The captain held a camera that he used to document this unusual and historic occasion, occurring on the tail end of the post-World War II Soviet Union.

The captain glanced at me and asked, "Do you want a picture?" He gestured towards the stately and unsmiling visages of the Soviet Bloc country officers. I pounced, "Sure!" Have I mentioned yet that I am not and never have been shy?

The captain stated something in Russian, and the officers were assembled into a line. I was placed in the center next to a stolid Russian infantry colonel whose name was even more challenging to pronounce than Vaishvila. The reality of this moment sunk in. I found myself flanked by Russian, Eastern German (Deutsche Demokratik Republik, (DDR), Czech, Hungarian, and Polish officials, including two major generals, all Soviets.

Nearly a year later, I received a personal letter from the young captain who had taken the picture. He apologized for the delay in sending it, citing challenges in permissions to release the photo through the White House. He provided a list of the names of the officers and their countries.

After eagerly opening the long-awaited envelope, I erupted in a snort of laughter. The image revealed a sea of barely smiling male faces interrupted by my starkly different countenance. There I stood, my blond hair spiked in the German style of the day, with the rest pulled up like the unruly yellow down of a wet duckling. All I was missing was a sparkling headband and leggings. This unfortunate style had no place with an Army uniform, but the regulations did not prevent it. Two enormous round rings of electric blue glasses graced my face. I guess I was trying to figure out my brand long before digital photography and selfie sticks; it took a photo with an unsuspecting group of Soviets to slap me into reality!

The 1980s was the height of the Jazzercize craze when spandex-squeezed figures boogied their way to better bodies with Richard Simmons. Once, our company First Sergeant decided to try something different, and for physical fitness (PT), he popped a Kathy Ireland video into the VCR. We military police bounced around laughing at ourselves because we were accustomed to running, pushups, sit-ups, and doctrinal-based exercises to help us grow in strength and flexibility. A flashy and flouncy workout set to music by the new artist Madonna was not exactly in our wheelhouse, and we laughed at ourselves and each other. Beyond my enormous glasses (the next pair were red, á la Sally Jessy Raphael), 80' fashions passed me by as I dealt with being a young mother and military officer in Germany. I don't feel like I missed out, as the 80s brought electric-colored spandex, legwarmers, and single fingerless glove accessories. Most unfortunately, a German "friseur" had gotten a hold of me and buzzed the top of my head, making me a quasi-dead ringer for "Stop the Insanity!" fitness guru Susan Powter. I even bleached the top platinum at one point before my temporary insanity was cured by sensibility.

Of course, as all trends do, the fashions would fade fast, leaving a generation of women doubly grateful for the lack of social media we experienced at the time. Memorializing any event involved traipsing to a drug store with a roll of film or a throwaway camera. This made a simple photo a big production, so many people didn't bother. "Why don't you have more pictures of when you were young?" was a question asked by so many kids of their parents who are my age (unless you owned a polaroid camera!).

I learned from the airplane hangar experience that if you are going to radically change your appearance, it might be a good idea to consider the profession you have chosen. It took a long time for my hair to grow back to a normal appearance. I still cringe when I see that historic photo and the juxtaposition of the significance of those Soviet officers in Cold War West Germany vis-a-vis my ridiculous attempt at fashion while in an Army uniform.

Over the years, the Army would undergo numerous updates to the regulations that would standardize hair, jewelry, makeup, and nail polish for women soldiers. The ghastly mint green uniform would be phased out. Until very recently, females had to wear male sizes of combat uniforms. Females of all shapes and sizes did their best with sizes like "small, medium' and 'medium, long" without hip room. When I became pregnant while on active duty, the "combat" pregnancy uniform either didn't exist or I wasn't issued it, and so I wore the Class B, which was more like a tent-like light green blouse with darker green skirts or trousers.

This leads me to mention pregnancy while I was still a second lieutenant, the lowest officer rank. It would appear that career-driven women, particularly military females, often held off on pregnancy and starting families while climbing the rungs of their professional ladders. This observation pertained to any job that mainly involved males but was evident particularly in the Army back then. Starting a career with pregnancy was, to say the least, not a career-enhancing move. Women were more likely to wait until later in their careers when they were established and had made it through various gates, whether training or deploying, before beginning their families. Starting a family was something I called the "Kiss of Death," but I did it intentionally.

When I became pregnant with my first child, I was still in Germany, and the year was 1988. My small unit, located outside of a military base and on the outskirts of Frankfurt, had not yet been issued standardized uniforms for physical fitness. These were gray sweatsuits with a large black ARMY across the T-shirt. Some batches of the shorts came out so short we called them "Daisy Dukes", after the old *Dukes of Hazzard* show in which Daisy sported mile-high short shorts at all times. Instead of the gray, we had yellow 70's style shorts with black trim that we referred to as "banana pants." We would pair these with our company t-shirt or a brown Army T-shirt. When I could no longer fit into this combination, I was instructed to wear whatever I wanted.

Physical training or PT in the Army was expected throughout most of the pregnancy but within certain restrictions spelled out in our medical profiles. At some point, we were ordered to work limited hours and cease appearing at those early PT formations. Most females wanted to show up if their pregnancies were healthy like mine. Those with morning sickness or other challenging pregnancy joys would try to demonstrate toughness by not vomiting or swaying queasily. Drinking ginger ale and eating saltines would become breakfast before the early morning formations at which my singular goal was not to fall out—it hurt not to be able to keep up.

I got as big as a whale. A serial runner and dieter, I was constantly famished. Resembling a ballooning beach ball, appointed with arms and legs, my body was a badge of honor as I continued to achieve in spite of the stereotypes, perceptions, and even snickers. Regardless of the self-deprecating jokes I would make, I was growing a tiny human who, after all, meant so much more to me than the changing size of my uniform.

During this first assignment, I was required to visit various field offices in our area of Western Germany. Arriving at military bases in places such as Wiesbaden, Fulda, and Darmstadt, the first thought on my mind was always to find food. "Does it have a Burger King?" I would ask when we planned our field office visits, much to the amusement of my platoon sergeant. I even had a driver, and he would get a huge grin, extremely amused by my line of questioning. In those days, Burger King seemed to be the only fast food we could find on the military bases in Germany. Only after I consumed fries and the largest burger I could find, would I set out to my duties. Later, when the movie *Fargo* came out, I could really relate to the pregnant burger-eating detective played by Frances McDormand.

The Kiss of Death was evident in my treatment by my then-chain of command. In fact, it was previously grounds for discharge, or, later, an optional decision to leave the military. Female soldiers have come a long way since those days; today, the Army emphasizes families and supports more extended maternity leave as well as other initiatives. Back then, I just knew that by placing family first, I would still land on my feet. Never mind that when I was pinned first lieutenant, I had gained 50 pounds!

In life, we are given a choice to follow trends or blaze our own trails. In my career, I have done both. Sometimes trends seem to work for a while, but ultimately, they are just a moment, a flash in the pan that fizzles out. There are leaders and there are followers, but there are also trailblazers. A true path to achievement is not a trend at all; it is a life path. It takes wisdom and courage to forge a direction that will produce longevity and a path for others.

Be intentional. Make decisions that will have an impact for those that follow your footsteps. Even a less popular path can become a roadway to a better direction.

Humans aren't camels.

Pause, and drink water.

# 4

## *Hydrate*

In Cold War Germany in the late 80s, there was always this sense of being on the brink of war. As much fun as most of us had touring castles and monasteries and drinking pure fresh beer, we also knew the gravity of the possibilities of escalated tensions with our Soviet-occupied neighbors. We were trained to identify any vehicle with license tags that had Soviet markings and report them to the nearest military police unit. Our training exercises were aimed at fending off attacks by the Russians in soon-to-be-outdated doctrinal waves of tanks assembling along the border with East Germany at what was called the Fulda Gap. Once, I visited a distant relative who lived in Wolfenbüttel, where Jaegermeister liqueur is made. The fences and guard towers were in plain sight, and we were not allowed to get close. It was a country split into two with the divided city of Berlin located in the occupied section to the east. A massive wall built after the war separated the city. The war had ended more for the USA, enjoying relative safety and new prosperity, than it did for those countries under Soviet occupation.

Officer Professional Developments in those days were events for unit officers that took on all different flavors, from educational to recreational. It is not a secret that for some of the all-male units, there would be evenings at various nightclubs involving strippers. My unit, to its credit, did not go to nightclubs; instead, we had an amazing visit to Berlin, a city steeped in rich history. The city had been divided and was occupied by England, France and the U.S. in the west and the Soviets in the east at the Yalta Conference in 1945. One of our MP units was assigned there and would host the event. We were to go behind the Iron Curtain and visit East Berlin! The culmination was the famous Checkpoint Charlie, the gateway to the east and west. The afternoon before our visit, we boarded the approved night train to Berlin, paperwork in hand.

The train lurched forward on the track, gradually settling into the rhythmic cadence of *click-clack, click-clack, click-clack* as it sped onward through the winding German countryside. I strained to see through the glassy window, my vision hampered by the inky black of the night sky. Shadows sped past, the looming ebony silhouettes rising and falling in the distance as if in a ghostly dance, turning in tune with the steady sound of the tracks. We traveled at night for a reason; we couldn't note our path or see into Soviet-occupied East Germany as we passed through it to arrive at our destination.

At five months pregnant, I was tired and thirsty. I had been offered the opportunity to stay back, but I said, "most absolutely, NO!" My silhouette had begun to round, reflecting the progress of the life growing inside me. The baby stretched and kicked from within, peacefully unaware of my discomfort. I marveled at the growing mound, still not grasping the reality of becoming a mother. However, it was also an increasingly uncomfortable experience as I gained far too much weight too quickly, and my body struggled to adjust. Each phase brought new challenges—morning sickness, swelling feet, painful joints, food aversions, and a seesaw of rapidly rising and falling emotions.

As the train sped through the night, I tried pointlessly to sleep on the narrow bunks assigned to each of us. My pregnancy magnified my thirst, and I found myself desperate for water, something I did not think to bring along. I had assumed it would be available.

In the Army, we are taught how important water is. Water is the essence of life, and, as such, we are taught to carry it everywhere with us. Beginning in basic training, the Army instructed us to carry two canteens on our standard-issued web belts. We also carried other items vital for survival: a collapsible entrenching tool, magazine clips for loading an M16 rifle, ammo pouches, and canteens. We females often struggled to make it all fit; however, the same was true for the more slightly built males! The Army institutionalized the value of drinking water in the form of mandatory water breaks (not to be confused with the legendary "smoke 'em if you got 'em" cigarette breaks, also an Army ritual until the connection with cancer became evident). Without water, we were rendered more ineffective than without all the other issued items.

Lying awake and uncomfortable on that train, I found myself wishing I was carrying my canteen. It seemed the rest of the world hadn't caught up with the Army's water drills. This was not a military train, and there were no concessions available. None. I was desperately thirsty, so I finally asked for some water. Scowling, the guard glared in response to my request before denying it. Doubtless, this was not the average transportation choice for women in my "delicate" condition.

Over the years I became religious in my need to have water with me at all times. While deployed in 2007, during the height of the "surge," we had easy access to water bottles. On U.S. facilities in Kuwait, Afghanistan, and Iraq, if we entered buildings, water bottles could be located anywhere, sometimes palletized and stacked as high as the ceiling. There were massive refrigerators purposed for cooling them. In arid environments, we sometimes were unaware of the amount we needed. I never took water for granted—it is life.

Speaking of storing water, I always had this fascination with camels. I photographed them and just loved how they could be seen lurching, albeit gracefully, in the desert in areas around Camp Arifjan, Kuwait. Camels seemed undaunted by the relentless heat and resulting need to quench thirst. I thought they were beautiful with their long eyelashes perched above soulful eyes and their loping awkwardness. When the Army brought in a camel for some off-duty riding pleasure at Camp Arifjan, I was thrilled! I had never seen one up close.

I credit my parents for my love for animals. We were raised with pets, and my mother loved to take me to the zoo. I joined the Ranger Rick Club and 4-H when I was in grade school. The colorful magazines I received from Ranger Rick were full of fun animal facts that captivated me and broadened my knowledge about creatures and critters. I was unprepared for my sadness when I saw how weary the old camel was. It appeared as if its best years were miles behind it, and it, too, could use a reviving drink of fresh water.

At first, I awaited my turn with great anticipation, but as soon as I awkwardly mounted this reluctant animal, the air immediately went out of my balloon. Arabian camels are tall majestic creatures with tawny coloring and a remarkable ability to go ten to fifteen days without water, the fat stored in their hump available as an energy source. This particular long-legged camel, as directed, would kneel to allow each new passenger to climb on, yet each time he did so, it was with a deep groan and what seemed to be a considerable amount of effort. The groan was unsettling.

I started to feel sorry for this tired camel, and as much as he groaned and moaned, I realized that I empathized with the poor beast. If he was hardy enough to survive days on end without water, he was strong enough to carry some individual troops around a large circle. Dressed in my combat uniform, I had to question whose idea it was to do this. As if some sort of lurching maniacal desert homecoming queen perched on my parade float, I suddenly felt embarrassed and ridiculous, and I couldn't wait to dismount. The camel circled the enclosure with me on its back, and I got my photo op before it creaked and grunted back to a kneel, depositing me on the ground, which I nearly kissed in relief. Those pictures exist, but they are staying at close hold, as I believe the morale boost missed its target, at least with me.

I was struck by the shocking juxtaposition of taking a camel ride while our service members were fighting and losing their lives in the wars in Iraq and Afghanistan. Camp Arifjan was considered a war zone in those times, yet it had a swimming pool, movie theater, and, yes, plenty of water. American men and women were fighting the global war on terrorism, and too many would return home in a flag-draped casket to the sorrow of heartbroken families and communities. The thought sobered me as I bid my final farewell to the groaning camel.

This realization gave me pause to reflect. In those rare quiet moments, I considered my surroundings, deriving lessons learned from my experience, drinking in the air, breathing deeply, and touching base with my God. How can I better the lives of others and balance that thought with caring for myself?

Years later, I held a demanding position at the Pentagon. A young captain worked there with me. He was positive and held great potential, always excelling at his work. There was something about his calm and reassuring manner that resonated with me;

surrounding ourselves with positive people was not something we could always choose.

One day, I was rushing from one meeting to the next and a little overwhelmed by another day of crammed schedules. The young officer stopped by my office to engage in a brief conversation. As he left my office, he turned to me and stated, "Drink water, Ma'am."

This simple statement held a powerful meaning that has stuck with me since that day. Anyone serving knows that the statement "drink water" can be both a command and a metaphor, like "take a knee." It can mean we need to pause and remember to check in with ourselves. As water is an essential element for preserving life, so is caring for our own needs. This gives us strength and energy to tend to those around us. As we are always reminded on flights, place your mask on your face first.

"Drink! Water!" was a command issued to us in training to remind us to hydrate. We were ordered to stop in our tracks to that directive. Yet, here I was, a relatively senior official at the Pentagon, being told the same thing by a young officer. He wasn't advising me actually to hydrate; he was letting me know that amid meetings and demanding responsibilities, I needed to take time to pause, check-in, and recharge my batteries. There is profound power in the pause. We become more in tune with others and more effective in our work when we practice the pause. Water is essential for life, as is the moment of restoration that comes when drinking it. We must be intentional about quenching our mental and physical thirst.

> Be present and point
> to what matters most
> in the moment.

# 5

# *Guilt*

The concept of work-life balance sometimes inaccurately promotes the idea that two major aspects of life can be perfectly prioritized: career and family. It's a paradox and a utopia that particularly working mothers strive to achieve, without realizing it can feel like an impossible mission.

Being a mother of two small children while serving in the Army was a daily struggle early on in my career. It was difficult to focus on the task at hand when the daycare was calling about a sick child! My struggle was to perform my daily missions with excellence and ensure my children received plenty of love along with their daily needs, including after-school activities. Sometimes the tasks felt more like spaghetti on a wall than linear objectives.

Tactical training involves mission sets and a (hopefully) clear objective. There are specified and implied tasks and fields of fire, so each team member knows what lane to stay in. Navigating the unspoken thought that pregnancy and motherhood weakens a soldier's effectiveness is a far more complex undertaking.

A senior rater brought me in for my annual rating and chatted with me. He was an older colonel or at least appeared that way to me at the time. I liked him. He credited me with recruiting female cadets at a traditionally male engineering university when I taught ROTC. That moment, he asked me with an air of sincerity, "What is your priority, Irene, the Army, or your children?" I automatically said, "Both, Sir!" He replied, "You can only have one." My days were peppered with thoughts of the kids, what was happening in school, and their well-being, and his comment made me sad. I wondered if he would ask any of my male counterparts the same question.

When my children were in high school, I worked for a general officer whose charisma was legendary. He was folksy when it suited him and a perfect gentleman to women during a time in my career when that style had become obsolete. (I used to joke about how the men let doors slam in my face before holding them. Then, when I was much older, it began to change). He had created a name brand before branding was even a thing, and everyone who had ever worked in his orbit had a funny story about him. He would grab a cigar and have select members of his staff stand under his favorite tree while he etched out his strategies. To be under that tree was an honor. On the other hand, his toughness was equally legendary, and he was known to reduce a briefing officer to a quibbling and drooling heap on the floor. If we worked hard and proved ourselves and our loyalty, he took outstanding care of us, and he was crucial in my path forward at the time.

Needless to say, I was eager to be a part of the "under the tree" group. I was at a point in my career where upward mobility to the next higher rank became much more difficult. My success would mean the difference between retirement or achieving full colonel, and I didn't want to retire. I continued to strive to balance being a wife and mother when my children were at a critical point in their teenage years—not the easiest thing to do.

On one such occasion, I was out shopping with my husband. We had driven together on a Sunday to a department store so that he could try on some new swim trunks. In my hand, I gripped the latest newfangled device in the dawning of the digital era—my Blackberry. Unlike popular flip phones, the Blackberry was a phone that boasted a full keyboard, a glowing toggle-ball roller, and rudimentary internet and email capacity. It would look like a dinosaur next to today's smartphones, but it was peak technology back then. Since only certain "key personnel" had a Blackberry in those days, it felt like a handheld badge of honor.

The Blackberry ushered in a new wave of phones that captivated the user in an inseparable addiction that was just dawning and resulted in the coining of the nickname "Crackberry." I was particularly proud of my "Crackberry" and didn't realize how much I checked it obsessively. I carried it everywhere I went because the general was notorious for calling on nights and weekends (or someone else who would connect him), and I was determined not to miss his call.

While my husband was in the dressing room that day, my Blackberry went off. I hollered at him, "I'll be right back," before dashing outside to take the call. On the line was the operations center to connect me with the general, demanding that I show up there and then, no questions asked.

I lurched into action and would have leapt into the car and driven off had I not realized that my husband had arrived in the same car. This was the only thing that kept me from leaving him behind in the dressing room as I rushed to respond to the general.

This was not a work-life balance. This was work outweighing life. That fight-or-flight mode, so important to a successful career, when sustained over time, can take a lasting toll on the physical and mental self. Heart pounding, mouth dry, I was a middle-aged mother who had just forgotten I had a husband and would race across town to receive my mission set for that Sunday afternoon.

This struggle was magnified in moments that I missed with my children. I wish that I had always gotten this right, but often, I did not. I was frequently torn between work and family, and the reality is that you can't be in two places at once. If you are physically there but mentally absent, you are not really there.

One Friday night, I sat in the bleachers of my son's high school football game with my "Crackberry" firmly clutched in my hand. As the daughter of immigrants, I wasn't raised with a strong connection to the sport of American football, but my husband loved it. He was a former Army player and a huge football fan, and he was overjoyed to have our son in the sport. My husband and I settled in to watch the game. As I watched, I clutched Mr. "Crackberry." It buzzed in my hand, and I thought I could check it quickly without missing any of the plays on the field.

I looked down to read a routine message when the crowd erupted in excitement. Their cheers grew in volume as I strained to see what all the commotion was about. My son had run an improbable touchdown. Soon thereafter he would leave football for another sport, and I had missed it. I had chosen to check my phone at the precise moment that he scored. I was physically in the stands but had not been present for this important moment.

I jumped up and down and celebrated the touchdown with everyone around me, pretending that I had seen it too, but deep inside, I felt like I was kneeling before a parenting judge. I knew that at that moment, I had prioritized a quick fix with my "Crackberry" over being present at the Friday night football game. No one was harder on me at that moment than myself.

I didn't tell my son or anyone about that, keeping it a silent guilty secret. It was not the first time, but the weight of trying to be the best at everything came crashing down on me that night. I wanted to be a successful military officer, but I also wanted to be a wonderful mother. Both things were important. Both held tremendous value to me. I couldn't help but think that the balance I was aiming for had shifted in the wrong direction. I was tired.

Over the years, time went by fast. I often reflected on my choices and asked myself, *How do I do it? How can I be in two places at once?* It wasn't possible. This is the plight of parents, not just serving in the military but everywhere, who hold demanding jobs by necessity or choice. It weighs all of us down as we tackle the wins and what feels like the losses.

If equilibrium between work and home life was an impossible balance, *where did that leave me?* While balance seemed impossible, pushing away guilt seemed even more. Each day and each moment, choices were placed in front of me. Army War College for a year at Carlisle, Pennsylvania, while missing our daughter's Prom Night. I would be sent somewhere when the kids had critical events in their lives. I had to build boundaries and run what the Army calls a Decision Matrix as I tried to navigate the minefield of what mattered most at that point in time.

Both my career and successfully raising children mattered. I was determined not to allow all of the noise around me to cause me to give up. I didn't want to take one step in the wrong direction. Sometimes we women are our own worst enemies, and I became used to Parent Teacher's Association parents implying that I was a lesser mother for my career ("I haven't seen you around!"). In the earlier days, when I went to new assignments, I tried not to let others know I had small children lest I be considered not committed to my work. If I let my guilt lead me, then I would always be playing catch-up.

I would try to compensate for the missed precious moments instead of moving on. This was not a winning strategy.

Things have changed a lot since I was a young mother in a career that at the time restricted women from most jobs. Today, women have more choices and much more institutional support as mothers. The struggles still remain, and decisions on whether to get off the career rollercoaster and get on the very different yet equally exhausting ride of being a full-time mom are always in conflict. Somehow, the kids are far more resilient than we think, and they usually end up just fine.

When my beloved mother's health became fragile, I turned down another move that was intended to build upon my career and allow me to become eligible for general officer. I turned it down, and consequently, I retired and had time to spend with my mother, who passed early the next year. Retirement felt like jumping off a speeding train, but in the end, I felt fortunate because it was a tough choice but the right one.

Proper training is essential for positive outcomes.

# 6

## Training

In 2003, I was assigned to the U.S. Army Reserve Command (USARC) at Fort McPherson, Georgia, a small but significant base located in Atlanta, Georgia. At that time, it housed the U.S. Army Central Command or ARCENT. Formerly known as the Third U.S. Army, it had been nicknamed "Patton's Army" for the famed military strategist and lightning-rod leader General George S. Patton. It has since been largely turned over to other entities. Fort McPherson also housed the four-star U.S. Forces Command, and several other units. I loved working at the USARC with its brand-new building flanked by a pond that held ducks, which some of us became very nurturing of and even named. If a duck disappeared, it would be an emotional event for me and ruin my whole day. Otherwise, the base had everything we needed and was near the airport, which was very convenient in a day before virtual meetings had become commonplace.

A lot of strategy and planning happened there, but my favorite was the massive Armed Forces Generation (ARFORGEN) conference, where senior Army leaders arrived from around the world and moved patch charts around on the big screen as rotations, both for training and combat, were planned in the near and not-so-near future. The patch charts depicted Army unit insignia. I was fortunate in 2005 to represent all of USARC training. I was one of only a few women in a massive auditorium, and I made connections that have lasted till this day.

I looked forward to making Fort McPherson my Army home for a while. Due to the promotion opportunities that existed there, I hoped this move would stabilize me and my family during my children's middle and high school years. I was hoping to be promoted and stay in place. My husband strongly believed that it was important for children not to have their high school years interrupted by moving, partly for the continuity of sports and other activities. I worried that a move at that point would be on my own, as so many military parents are forced to do if they are moved during a period in which their families want to stabilize. I desperately hoped this move would allow me to remain should I be promoted to lieutenant colonel. For the record, no promotion is a guarantee, and nothing can be taken for granted.

## Training

When I first arrived, I was placed in the position of managing all military police individual reclassification training. This meant that I planned and budgeted for the training that converted Army Reserve and National Guard soldiers from their operational specialty to military police. Reclassification would occur for a number of reasons, including desire, a move to an area that doesn't have positions open in a career field, or needs of the Army as was the case during this period of wartime in the Middle East. Whether it was a Guard or Reserve soldier reclassifying, the training was conducted by one of several large Army Reserve training units. I was responsible for coordinating with training officers around the Army Reserve, and I have made enduring friendships as a result. I loved that job due to the satisfaction it gave me and my stroke of luck at having an amazing boss who believed in me. Water a flower, and it blooms.

One day, I was summoned into the three-star commanding general's office without notice. A somber weight seemed to rest on the room as I stood at attention, looked at him, and listened as the words *Abu Ghraib* began to surface. I didn't know yet what had just occurred at Iraq's so-named U.S. military detainee facility, but I sensed it was very bad. I hadn't heard about the atrocities committed there by several U.S. soldiers because the news did not travel as quickly then as it does now. The general called me in because the question hung in the room: how and when were these soldiers trained, and what went so terribly wrong? What mistakes did we make, and how can we even begin to repair the damage?

The events exposed at Abu Ghraib were horrific violations of almost every human right imaginable. Located west of Baghdad, under Iraqi control, the prison had a notorious past reputation as a place of torture and execution of political prisoners, confirmed through the excavation of Saddam Hussein-era mass graves. When the U.S. Army briefly assumed control of the Abu Ghraib facility after the invasion of Iraq in 2003, they made it into a detention facility. That same year, horrific acts involving the torture of detainees by a few guards hit the news media. Exposure of this information stirred appalled outrage as our nation reacted in horror.

I had barely arrived in my new job managing Army Reserve military police training. As such, I was one of several officers called into the commander's office that day to dissect the history of the training and readiness of the involved military police units. It was on us to attempt to determine what went so devastatingly wrong at Abu Ghraib and what needed to take place immediately to ensure that it never would happen again.

## Training

Over time, the facts revealed that due to vast shortages of military police soldiers needed for the Global War on Terror, or GWOT as it was called then, some military police units had been "cobbled" together with soldiers who had never met one another, much less trained together. Due to a number of (preventable) reasons, these military police units were insufficiently vetted and inadequately or improperly trained without oversight and then sent overseas. In addition, in the GWOT's early years, Army Reserve units had deployments extended for up to two years in these austere and volatile environments. The long deployments caused morale issues and hurt families. All combined, the result was a weak link that broke very publicly.

Following these issues, Abu Ghraib was turned back to the Iraqi government. The Army Reserve added unit (or collective) training to my portfolio of responsibilities the next year. I recognized the gravity of this task and was grateful to work alongside the best boss possible. He had a vision to build the first-ever large scale joint training exercise for Army Reserve units of all branches.

We saw an obvious need to have more realistic collective training involving multiple units with increased oversight in order never to experience again what had recently happened. Together we planned for and stood up Army Reserve widescale training exercises with names like Desert Warrior and Desert Justice. The result was outstanding training for units having mutually supporting missions to come together and train in realistic environments. For realism there were joint assets, initially in the form of a parachute regiment from Canada. This training was held at Fort Bliss, Texas.

While there, I met with the English-speaking commander of a French-speaking parachute unit. There was an issue that I needed to address, and a meeting was scheduled. Imagine my surprise when amid this imposing group of a rugged all-male unit of paratroopers, a female commander emerged sporting a ponytail and an (approximately) five-month pregnancy! I was stunned and filled with complete admiration. This impressive woman walked with authority and— even with her very evident pregnancy bump— was commanding their unquestioning respect in a way that I had not experienced in my time in the late 80s.

I admired the environment in which this commander was serving and which held her as a full equal. Pregnancy back in my day seemed to be viewed as a weakness, complete with the barely audible occasional snickers, while I carried out my duties and increased daily in girth. Yet, this commander held her bearing and commanded the respect I hadn't realized in my day. Thankfully, growing a family has been normalized today, but back then, around 2005, I was inspired by this female commander's no-nonsense and nothing-to-see-here approach as she carried out her duties. Pregnancy clearly wasn't sidelining her career. I so was impressed, and it motivated me to think differently about myself.

This encounter with a female commander was exciting, but it was just one memorable moment within the more considerable significance of the whole exercise. This exercise was the first ever for the Army Reserve, leading to an entire series of exercises after that. Other branches of the Army Reserve traditionally held separate exercises, but what we did with this desert exercise began a new era of training that allowed for different specialties to train in realistic environments side by side as the active Army had always done before. Ultimately, we gained a seat at the National Training Center (NTC) in Fort Irwin, California, one of the several combat training centers in the Army. It was a privilege to have had a role in this endeavor.

At that time, Army training had evolved from the World War II legacy doctrine that my peers and I had studied in the early 80s. We were trained to understand conventional warfare involving large Russian unit movements with tanks and soldiers, all named *Ivan*. *Ivan* was as common a term when describing Soviet forces as "Tommies" were in World War I and II to reflect the British; neither term meant as flattery.

The NTC institutes training that reflects emerging Army doctrine and continuous lessons learned. It immerses units into realistic training environments similar to areas of the Middle East due to its location in the high Mojave desert. It is astounding to me to see how much Russia faded into the background of American consciousness as the Soviet-made wall came down in Berlin in the late 80s, and the wars in Iraq and Afghanistan ramped up after 9/11. The NTC responded quickly by hiring role players with critical language skills that had evolved into Arabic, Farsi, Dari, Pashtun, and others.

Today, Russia has come roaring back with force as an existential threat to Western democracy, and training reflects the response to that threat.

Proper training is essential to mission readiness. The travesty of Abu Ghraib in 2003 was horrific yet avoidable. Had our soldiers appropriately trained together in preparation for a rotation, we could have identified problems and fixed them early and instead focused on our collective strengths. As leaders, we couldn't change the past, but we could ensure that the Army learned from its lessons to prevent something like that from happening again in the future.

In leadership, proper training methods must be implemented and reinforced to be prepared and avoid future disasters. "Old Blood and Guts" General George S. Patton once said, "A pint of sweat will save a gallon of blood." Training hard saves lives. Time and effort to get it right must be expended to protect ourselves, our soldiers, and our reputation of honor that the United States strives to uphold in our own country and while deployed in others.

A tiny lightning bug,

when surrounded by others,

can spark an illumination.

# 7

## *Shine*

Laughter filled the streets of my Arlington, Virginia, childhood neighborhood at dusk as children gleefully captured fireflies within their cupped hands and roamed the street until our parents called us in, often after dark. These were the innocent days of unsupervised childhood play that many of us experienced in the 70s. We climbed trees, played "Ghost in the Graveyard," and hid ourselves from each other in the neighbors' yards. We were safe, or at least we all believed we were, and enjoyed our completely unscheduled freedom. Back then, we thought we were safe without seatbelts, sunscreen, hand sanitizer, or bicycle helmets. Some of us like to reflect somewhat sardonically on how we even survived.

I loved fireflies and still do, but I don't see them much anymore. These iridescent creatures, once caught, were unwittingly placed in small glass jars with holes punched into the lids. We enjoyed our makeshift nightlights that glinted and glowed in their golden flashing luminescence. I loved all critters in general and couldn't bring myself to harm or restrain these wonderous lightning bugs, symbolic of warm spring and summer evenings. However, I watched the other children delight in this childhood rite of passage.

As a sworn Ranger Rick member, I made it my mission to protect these glowing glories, not to mention spiders and all manner of bugs. I am certain the other neighborhood children didn't understand my heart for these insects, and no one attempted to try. That didn't deter me from standing firm in my position. Today, pesticides and overpopulation have threatened my favorite bugs, so nostalgic of my youth. I was prescient in my concern for the little guys.

In some areas of the state of Mississippi, reside species of fireflies that blink in synchronicity, turning a symphony of glowing lights into a well-timed flashing cadence of simultaneous blinks. It is a rare phenomenon that is magical to witness. The twinkling sky filled with glowing bugs flashing in unison, like a string of strobing Christmas lights, is a wonder that I am told draws curious visitors from far and wide to admire.

Camp Shelby was also located in Mississippi, yet the bugs had nothing to do with my visit. Not even close. I was a military police training manager for the Army Reserve, and a few of us traveled there to look for a new home for military police and other reclassification training. A critical shortage of military police and transportation officers needed to be filled quickly and efficiently for growing requirements in Iraq and Afghanistan at the height of the wars during a period called "The Surge." In the end, National Guard field artillery units were selected for conversion to military police to fill those needs.

It was critical that the training met all physical requirements for these new units; and to do that effectively, we had to choose a military location that could handle the load and had the right facilities. Along with other field grade officers (in this case, majors), coincidentally all female and each with their own similar agendas, I traveled to some far-flung places to assess the feasibility of the potential for a new training location.

These trips, plain and simple, were fun. There was something to each base, but I really liked Camp Shelby. The base had a natural beauty in Mississippi that brimmed with southern hospitality. The garrison commander greeted us with a warm welcome that left a lifelong impression. Of course, there was a direct benefit to making a good impression on those of us evaluating the base for requirements. The communities surrounding the bases were bolstered by businesses that the base brought in, along with an increased population that pumped money into the local economy. It was incredibly advantageous for a base to bring in business in the form of additional training opportunities and the resulting hundreds of troops.

We left the base at the end of our first day at Camp Shelby to get something to eat. I suggested we go out the back gate, near where some eateries were located.

One of the majors with me stated matter-of-factly, "We can't go out the back gate."

"Why not?" I asked naively.

"It isn't safe for me there," she said.

I looked at her blankly, not understanding her meaning.

"Everyone in my community knows that you don't go out of the back gate," she said.

"Wow," I replied, stunned as her meaning became clear.

That moment opened my eyes to the challenges that minorities faced within the Army then. I had been so focused on my personal uphill battle as a woman in the Military Police Corps in the 80s and 90s that I hadn't considered what this major was experiencing. She was fighting to break barriers and overcome challenges occurring in her daily military life— not just as a woman, but also as a minority woman. This was a humbling realization for me, and all I knew was that it made me feel angry. We did not go out the back gate.

This event served to jolt me into awareness of what others not like me had to deal with back then, and it resonated with me and humbled me. I learned to ask questions and observe so that I could empathize, try to understand, and work to do what I could to make a difference. Understanding others' perspectives is a critical step toward cultural change. Simply articulated, my travel companion's frankness and matter-of-fact manner of stating her reality really grabbed me.

In my early days in the military, my male counterparts were often unsure how exactly to treat me. We females often felt like we had to work harder not to rise to the top but just to stay even. We shook our heads when news broke of horrific scandals that even had names: "Aberdeen Scandal" and "Tailhook Scandal." I couldn't change a culture alone, but I could model all the strength I could muster and the humility and compassion needed to make positive changes for the future. I could impact my immediate environment and treat all people with dignity and respect, which is what I did and still do.

Leadership involves listening and understanding that all people have different perspectives based on their life experiences and culture. These different perspectives are a valuable part of what builds a healthy community. A diversity of voices creates a thriving culture. Sometimes it is even harder to listen to what someone is not saying. I learned to listen carefully, ask questions, find common ground, and embrace differences, forging relationships that last to this day.

At the Army War College, every group, called a seminar, had two International Fellows that studied alongside us for that year. I enjoyed getting to know some of them as they arrived from all around the world. The gentlemen from the United Arab Emirates used to greet me by saying, "How is your family?" I was used to the "How are you?" greeting we Americans use, and it took me by surprise. I could appreciate the value that families held in his culture, and also, what a nice way to find common ground because everyone everywhere belongs in a family.

The culture of the Army has changed over the years. Army Values are taught and reinforced and a brotherhood includes the sisterhood that transcends the past. It will continue to change, but many overlook the truth that change is often made on the micro level before it moves to the macro. Each of us has the opportunity to shine our light, hoping that we can inspire others.

Once, I had a job where I took care of a general officer's correspondence. I found a letter for him to sign that expressed sympathy for a major's son's death, and it struck me. I picked up the phone to the major to express my own deep sympathy, and he told me what had happened. I got to know him a little. He later said to me, when he was in the Pentagon, that I had a way of making people feel like they were the only person in the room.

This perspective came with hard work, lessons learned, and maturity, as the realization dawned on me early that I am not the only one who has struggled. We focus so much on our own path. I learned my voice was being heard and could have an impact. Later I used this skill to help numerous others, some of whom were young and just starting out in their military careers and others who were going through issues in their transition out of the Army. Sometimes all anyone needs is a little light and comfort to shine on them to flourish and grow.

We can learn from Mississippi lightning bugs who glow stronger and brighter in unison. We can do the same in our own way, sparking change in our organizations and creating a glowing path for others who come behind us.

Cats land on their feet.

Sometimes you don't,

but you can always

get back up.

# 8

## *Landings*

"You are like a cat, Ma'am. Throw you up in the air, and you always land on your feet." This was an unusual compliment early in my career from someone who first recognized something in me that I did not know I had. Resilience. Life is full of rough spots and ups and downs, but rising from these hard landings is the key to moving forward and, ultimately, success.

In the Army and in life, I literally and figuratively had my share of hard landings. Hard landings are not something that anyone seeks out. Many of us hope for a life cushioned with soft landings, but the reality is that the tough ones help us to learn and grow, even when nothing makes sense.

The mammoth Lockheed C-130 Hercules has long been the workhorse of the American military. Initially used for cargo, troop, and medevac transport, it still does all those things but is also used by all the services for tactical airlifting or placing resources at a precise location. In 2007, the first time I was on a tactical flight poised to make a tactical landing, I flew from Kuwait to Baghdad in a C-130.

I found myself uncomfortably crammed in a seat on the side of the plane, recalling that the last time I had flown in one of these beasts, it had been to jump out of it. I loved the exhilaration of jumping; it had been like leaping into an unknown void of air currents that buoyed me for those few moments of joy, but all things come to an end at some point, and that had to, as well.

On one particular jump, I made a critical mistake. I was so awestruck by the beauty of the vast horizon that I dreamily watched as the tree line rapidly rose toward me. We were not airborne long enough for daydreams. Mesmerized, I landed faster than anticipated, my boots striking the ground with force as I made a poor landing, one that broke one foot and sprained my other ankle. Unable to help myself up, I lay pinioned to the ground by the force and the damage of my fall. I couldn't get up even as a noncommissioned officer angrily barked at me to move. Eventually, I did get up but needed help, and it ruined my day as well as the next four or so months. The Army gave me crutches—so how do you not put weight on either foot? That was a hard landing. I paid for that moment of daydreaming for life, as old injuries tend to come back to haunt us as we get older.

Some fifteen years later, I found myself in the same type of aircraft headed from Kuwait to Iraq. This particular tactical landing on the C-130 would not involve me jumping out. I was along for the ride but increasingly nervous as we prepared our approach. Baghdad was a warzone; as we neared it, all the lights went out to avoid unnecessary attention. It went dark. A tactical landing involves flying at much higher altitudes to avoid anti-aircraft weaponry, and in environments at risk for small arms fire, landings are unique to combat zones because it are conducted in a rapid helix type of maneuver.

As the plane began its descent, it spun at a high rate of speed, jarring and jolting us in a choppy spiraling maneuver that had several of the soldiers on board grabbing their issued bags. Some had been through this many, many times, but I was not one of them. The landing hit with a bang and sudden roughness as we were hastily thrust off the plane. Running off the tarmac, we were rushed to a structure resembling a wooden sidewalk. The aircraft had stirred up dirt and dust, and I choked on it, thinking, *this is Baghdad*. What a far cry from the luxurious airport terminals back home at Dulles International Airport or Reagan National that I was used to for my work at the Pentagon and in Washington, D.C.

I was ushered later that night to a tent where I could get a little sleep. Helicopters made sleep difficult. This temporary residence was a general-purpose medium-sized tent (we called them GP Mediums) with a cot for sleeping. Cots were all lined up, but none were occupied, so I had the tent to myself.

They showed me the porta-potties lined up in a row adjacent to the units housing sinks for teeth brushing. There were four to six sinks, so it was important to brush quickly due to the line that formed up. Everything was well-maintained and surprisingly very clean, and we had it relatively good there.

I learned a lot from visiting bases like Camp Victory and Camp Cropper. The important lesson I learned from my rough landings stands out to me the most: Sometimes life comes at you hard. I didn't fully understand this concept initially, but years later experienced this in a trifecta of changes that occurred all at once. I was to turn fifty, retire from the military, and lose my mother all within one year.

Fifty is a milestone that often signals a turning point, physically, mentally, and emotionally. It is a natural prompt to take stock of where you have come from and determine a path for the future. Yet, this can be tricky, facing an entrance to a new era of the unknown. For me, it took some adjusting to feel comfortable with who I was and where I was going as I approached that time in my life.

Becoming fifty would have been less of a transition had it not been so intricately tied to my retirement from the Army. I loved the Army; by then, it had become a beloved and inextricable part of my personal fabric. I loved the work, the camaraderie, and the collection of many incredible people I had been privileged to work beside. The Army made me, in a sense, who I was and, in part, had become a large part of my identity. I felt like I was part of a large family. Leaving the military felt like being thrown off a speeding train and onto the side of the road. The train never stops, and you are left lying there trying to figure out where you are.

It wasn't only me that felt left behind when retiring from the military. Many of my peers, colleagues, and friends have echoed similar sentiments. For most of us, the transition is hard. It is jolting to go from a fast-paced environment that doesn't pause, slow, or stop into the civilian world, as we call it, where any structure or schedule must be set by ourselves to keep us moving. It can feel very much alone. Suddenly, where was the daily camaraderie and the mutual regard that comes from having accomplished really tough hurdles together? I felt lost in the transition.

To separate from the military was a severing of something I held dear, but losing my mother soon thereafter was devastating. My mother and I had been incredibly close, and I felt her loss keenly. I took her death incredibly hard. Life's landings could be rough, but ultimately, as my platoon sergeant said so long ago, I landed on my feet. I couldn't just lay there as the metaphorical train rushed past me. I had to get on a different train—one heading toward a new future, embracing my post-military life, keeping active, and leveraging the skills and abilities I had gained in life so far. Combining fifty years of life experience, military tenacity, and the loving feeling only a mother can give, I invested in the resilience of rebuilding and sculpting a future on the foundations that I had already built.

Feeling adrift, I chose to land on my feet. I returned to my Lutheran faith—the multiple moves had taken their toll on my church participation. My husband and I took the time to build the home that we would eventually retire to. I never really retired. Instead, I busied myself with a new career in the federal government, began volunteering in earnest, and celebrated my grown children's accomplishments and life choices.

In life, it is essential to know that hard landings are only temporary. They may knock you down, but you will rise up, almost always, with help from others. When jolted by the brutal reality of a harsh landing or a devastating event, it is important to know that things will get better; they always do, especially if you have faith.

Sometimes we choose our battles, but often they pick us.

# 9

## *Choose*

Choose your battles. Sometimes they will choose you. Throughout my career, but particularly in the earlier days, sometimes daily comments or micro-events caused me to stop and wonder if I needed to act or let something go. (Wait, did he just say that???) What I should address or not address regarding the treatment of myself or women in general resulted in my having to pick my battles, so to speak. I had the presence of mind to know that things would change eventually, and I knew I had to be wise in what I chose to align myself with versus champion against. For the most part, I focused on the tasks in front of me and stayed out of the politics of it all.

The United Service Organizations (USO) has brought live entertainment to the troops since World War II. Celebrities of all kinds volunteered to bring shows to them, including Bob Hope, Marilyn Monroe, Danny Kaye, Mickey Rooney, and so many more. The shows gave troops a slice of home and a morale boost as a respite and to help them forget, even for a moment, the harsh reality of war or simply long separations from home. This was and still is a truly incredible organization that champions, cares about, nurtures, and entertains servicemen and women around the globe.

In Germany in the '80s, a local commander had his own version of how to entertain his exhausted unit (minus the junior enlisted) after long, wet, cold field exercises conducted in Hohenfels, Germany. He decided to commandeer the camp noncommissioned officer club one evening and brought in strippers. All staff sergeants and above from this unit were mandated to come. Reports of this event never quite made it out of the club that night, except for the wives of those men who were honest about it! Increasing numbers of women in more combat support roles (we weren't in combat roles yet) back then shed light on these and other similar incidents, and eventually, over time, they disappeared. Evidently, the commander heard about it, but not because of the strippers; instead, he was reprimanded for commandeering the noncommissioned officers club!

Officer Professional Development (OPD) was a different story but somewhat related as it promoted another form of morale boost. Officers from around the unit and its higher headquarters could get away and see and learn something new. Sometimes it involved a "staff ride" where there were visits to battlefields accompanied by historians or other sites where we could walk the grounds and learn about what, why, and how battles unfolded there. Germany's neighboring countries were rich with WWII battlefields and battle monuments.

On one such OPD, my unit took us on a study of divided Berlin and behind the Berlin Wall, where we could see first-hand what Cold War communism looked like. West Berlin was a fascinating city, but East Berlin felt post-apocalyptic: no one in the streets, cameras on high poles whirring in every direction, and forced smiles as we ate in a "high quality" restaurant where everyone, looking miserable, stared at us. We seemed to be the only diners as if it was a stage show put on just for us. The decor was elegant and from a different era, but the food was very sparing and not good. These memories will stay with me forever. They helped put into perspective the great freedoms Americans enjoy in all aspects of our daily lives.

A dining-out was another social event in a formal setting where units got together and brought spouses to enjoy a fun night of fellowship and camaraderie. These evenings provided a forum to escape the work environment; there was good food, a speaker, and dancing afterward. I particularly looked forward to attending my first dining-out as a married junior officer in Germany.

While many of the women arrayed themselves in sophisticated and elegant gowns, I had an option and chose to wear my uniform. I was very proud of my uniform; occasions to wear it were few. In my dress blue uniform, I made an extra effort to apply makeup and even managed to coax my now growing-out ridiculous blond mullet into a professional style. Little pearls went in my earlobes, one of several authorized earrings exclusively worn with the dress uniform or the less formal "Class A" uniform. Earrings were absolutely never allowed in the camouflage utility uniform. Keeping lipstick at the ready for touch-ups and proudly holding my new husband's arm, I glided into the highly anticipated event.

As usual at these events back then, the beer and wine flowed freely, and I happily floated along, listening half-heartedly as speeches began. Talking with table guests was more fun! The speaker, a general officer, began by emphasizing the importance of spending quality time with family. It was a cautionary speech against being a workaholic. Since my husband and I were always so busy working that we didn't see each other much, my ears perked up to focus more intensely on what he was saying.

Suddenly, the general asked, "How well do you think you know your wife? Do you know her likes and dislikes? Do you know her bra size?" He continued with that line of thought like it was nothing. For some reason, that comment made me feel just plain angry. How could we wives possibly be identified this way in such a formal setting? And me in a uniform, to boot. I picked that battle to fight. I noisily pushed back my chair, stood up, and walked out of the room. I was making a statement. My husband had to scramble to follow me out as I stalked out, fuming.

"Now, what does that have to do with anything?" I vented to my husband, incensed. "I don't ask you about your jockstrap size, and THAT certainly wasn't addressed!!" I was angry at the flip sexism of it all, reducing wives to a bra size and not taking into account that half the room were women; it was pure disrespect. And condoned! There didn't seem to be any recourse.

I have had the distinct pleasure of working over the years with women who made much bolder, broader statements than my small show of theatrics at the dining-out that evening many years ago. Typically, I was not one of them. That evening, I was not looking for a fight, but one found me anyway, and I was mad enough to make a statement. I am proud of myself for doing that. On the other hand, small victories could result in the dreaded label of 'whiney" or, even worse, troublemaker.

Another incident occurred in the mid-90s when as a senior captain, I taught Army ROTC at a university. One summer I found myself at Fort Lewis, Washington, as a member of a tactical team that evaluated ROTC cadets going through their summer leadership training. The training and evaluations would serve as a focal point for an overall assessment of their potential as soon-to-be Army officers. We were the cadre and, as such, stayed in a barracks area apart from the cadets. Late one afternoon while off duty, I walked through the cadre area. A master sergeant known for being humorous pulled a line from Saturday Night Live and shouted down from the window of the building's third story, "My name is INGA, and I'm from SCHVEEEEEDEN!!" I looked up and laughed out loud. Sweden and Lithuania were separated by the Baltic sea as well as by history, language and culture; this was some version of a stereotype. That day, I chose not to pick a battle over his comment.

I usually didn't want to rock the boat or make waves. I typically kept my head down (and powder dry, as the saying goes) and worked hard, trying to avoid confrontation or controversy. How could I advance if I had a fresh complaint every day? I was not raised that way. However, this did not mean that I didn't have boundaries or an expectation for treatment with dignity and respect as we all do. I knew my own limits.

There are times when we will enter a fray to advocate for what is right. Other times while in our formal wear, looking forward to a night of wine and dancing, the fray comes to us. Be prepared to fight but think first and be equally prepared not to.

Modesty is a state of mind.

# 10

## *Modesty*

Modesty means something different to everyone and is steeped in tradition and culture. Modesty manifests itself in clothing and comportment that carefully follows norms established by society, religious leaders, parents, and other groups. In the late 60s and 70s, men and women broke up those norms by trading in their parents' formal dress codes; and fashions like bikinis, spaghetti straps, bare mid-drifts, miniskirts, and short shorts exploded onto the American scene. Not everyone was on board.

For soldiers, some aspects of modesty went completely out the window upon initial entry. Women showered together, dressed together, trained, and sweated together. There was no time to be self-conscious. The men did it; we could too. We all knew each other's menstrual cycles due to the necessity of time-eating extra steps needed to deal with them, and we experienced the folklore wisdom of having all of our cycles synch up when we were close together for a period of time (so to speak). Even when fully exposed, there was a sense of coverage within our respect for one another—a shared sense of protection. We had our issues that our male counterparts would never have to deal with.

When I first arrived at Fort Dix, New Jersey, our foot locker displays had to be identical and were subject to stringent inspections by the drill sergeants. Our T-shirts and clothing that did not require a hanger were carefully displayed in a manner we all knew as dress-right-dress. That meant we each had to have six bras, all nested neatly within each other as they merrily lay side-by-side. The problem was if we arrived without six identical bras, we were marched to the PX (post exchange, or shop) to buy six identical bras. Calamity! Sports bras were barely even invented, nor were they available, and it was a mess trying to find one of those pearl white dainty lingerie items that could account for the impressive variety of female measurements. There seemed to be four size options on the shelves. I had to select the smallest ones, which were all too small, given the next size up felt like I could put my entire head into a cup. I always cringed when my tiny bras were inspected. I could have fit maybe a golf ball in the cups. The straps strangled me daily, and females who train in sports bras today can thank the pioneers who first invented them (and yes! hold the patent).

## Modesty

Recently, I attended a conference at the U.S. Patent and Trade Office and had a tour of the Inventor's Hall of Fame. I laughed out loud to see a very early prototype of a sports bra: two jockstraps sewn together!! That's when I learned that several women pioneers invented the sports bra in the late 70s. Runners rejoiced! But they hadn't made their way to the Fort Dix PX yet. Inventors Linda Lindhal, Polly Smith, and Hinda Miller, I salute you and bow to you in gratitude, along with all the women who helped turn JogBra into a $17 billion-a-year industry.

Over time, some institutional assaults on modesty were phased out when their implications were realized. In those early days of my jump school training, a practice occurred to avoid heat casualties after heavy exercise under the scorching hot rays of the Georgia sun. This involved all trainees removing their "blouses"—camouflage utility tops that were worn over T-shirts—in order to be cooled down from the spray of a large hose. It was a little bit like running a gauntlet, and the soaking spray was a welcome respite from the blazing, unrelenting heat. Males and females ran through the spray without any thought of it. However, the respite was short-lived as our soaking shirts clung to our bodies, invoking images of wet T-shirt competitions and prompting ill-concealed entertainment by our male trainee counterparts. Checking our modesty at the door was one thing but respect another, and the benefits of cooling off evaporated quickly in the aftermath. This practice was discontinued.

Semi-annual weigh-ins were the stuff of legends. Two times each year, almost always in October and March, all soldiers took (and still do) standardized physical fitness tests followed by the sometimes-dreaded step onto a medical scale. The Army Physical Fitness Test (APFT), recently changed in its entirety, consisted of push-ups, sit-ups, and a two-mile run. I was very fortunate that sit-ups and pushups were easy for me, and I was a runner dating back to middle school so I enjoyed taking the tests. Not everyone did. It seems that body type has something to do with a proclivity for sit-ups and pushups; for example, long arms or a long wingspan (as they say in football) resulted in more time and effort to lower the body and break the plane as required when executing a pushup.

And the weigh-ins! Particularly as we aged and natural weight crept on as an inevitable part of life, they could prove daunting. At the scale, we lined up for our turn, surrounded by bosses, peers, and subordinates as our numbers were called off. Our height and weight were a matter of public record, like it or not.

We had weigh-ins after the APFT, and they easily could result in an awkward experience for both males and females. If the prescribed weight was exceeded, out came the tape measure to measure body fat percentages, also a pass/fail endeavor. The charts made sense to an athlete but, conversely, did not favor all body types. The well-muscled, heavier soldiers, both male and female, often didn't pass their weigh-ins and were sent to the tape test line in another area.

The tape test involved measurements taken around the neck, waist, and hips for females and the neck and waist for males. For both males and females, it was not an advantage to have a too-small neck. For women, hip size could be the difference between pass and fail. (Hips are very genetic. I have my grandmother's). These tape tests were relatively new when I first came in and were still in effect until very recently, rife as they were with human error and endless complaints throughout the years. Weight could destroy an opportunity or even a career, and so the weigh-in was often an anxiety-inducing experience.

One summer, I was sent as a TAC (tactical) officer to Fort Lewis, Washington, where ROTC training was occurring. Somehow while there, I was tasked with administering the tape test to the males who did not pass the weight standards. It was immediately after the PT test, and the long line seemed endless as male after male walked up to me, pulling up now-sweaty Army T-shirts, exposing their midsections for me to measure with a tape. I had to awkwardly adjust my stance with each male based on their height. There was no modesty for them as each belly was presented. I felt like I was drowning in an endless sea of male midsections. Sweaty belly after sweaty belly, check! Don't suck in your gut! Exhale! Don't flex your neck! Flexing necks was very common for the small necks. This went on for hours due to the number of cadets training. I had the passing thought that I felt bad that all these men had to display their bellies to me, and that made me feel bad for them.

I'm sure it was far more important to them to pass than to overthink the process. I was never taped but experienced my own weight-related drama. Just entering the Army at eighteen, the weight tables at that time had what seemed to be an unnatural standard for my height and age: 126 pounds was the limit. I stood on the scale one summer at a trim 123 pounds. The master sergeant sucked air through his teeth and said upon my weigh-in, "Vaishvila (one of the few who could pronounce it), you need to lose some weight off those HIPS."

His offhand comment led me into a flurry of panic. I was three pounds under the weight standard at the start of my career! Those three pounds were the difference between failing and passing the weigh-in. Other than drinking TAB soda, the only diet drink available back then, I wasn't used to worrying about my weight. I was a prolific runner and extremely fit. I even lifted weights, something less common for women in the early 80s. Aside from my Burger King binges when pregnant years later, I maintained a relatively healthy diet. Feeling fat-shamed was something new that had me scurrying off to nutritionists who (ridiculously) put me on diets, and the Fear of the Scale was born. Those weight standards were changed a few years later and have been updated several times since then.

I was a self-starter, and regardless of the Army's standards, my best competition was with myself. Every APFT I took was a self-imposed competition with my past record. I wanted to push harder and achieve more than the previous records. One year, I didn't meet my own standards. I had a tough winter, and when I took the test that March, I had gained a noticeable amount of weight.

I was still barely within Army weight standards, but the noncommissioned officer weighing me looked at my last weight and compared it to my current weight before stating loudly, "Damn, ma'am, you've been eating too many donuts." This was not only a dig at my weight but also a dig at being a military police officer. This fed the insulting narrative of law enforcement officers sitting in cars outside of Dunkin Donuts. I bit my tongue, which sometimes felt like hamburger meat—not a battle worth picking that day. My struggle that day was real as it was for soldiers who donned weight loss suits meant for wrestlers and sat in saunas for days before a weigh-in.

Don't get me wrong. I embraced the test and the standards, but empathized with those who struggled due to body type, medical conditions that emerged later in their careers, and other reasons. Pregnancy weight can be a bear! The APFT recently was overhauled so as to not differ between males and females, and the height and weight standards are being carefully considered.

Upon reception at basic training, we all received duffle bags filled with issue clothing, and we had to forfeit our civilian clothing along with our modesty. There was the shared experience that we were all in it together. It was harder for some of us females to embrace the communal nature of what we called personal hygiene time than for others. But we worked to make it as seamless as possible. There would be a time and a place to return to our private selves.

To understand the past

is to prepare for

the future.

# 11

## *Repeat*

Afghanistan is sometimes referred to as the Graveyard of Empires. Its lands, rich with natural resources and strategically located at the crossroads of Asia and Central Europe, have been repeatedly invaded and conquered throughout history. Modern history has seen British rule, ruling kings, a pro-Soviet President, a Russian invasion lasting ten years, and a president and his failed government that has today collapsed into the hands of the Taliban, an Islamic militia first formed in 1995. In the 20th century, Afghan women have borne the greatest burden of the oppressive regimes that destroyed their human rights and basic civil liberties. When reinstated, their liberties were stripped again. Patterns emerged, and patterns repeated themselves.

In the early '70s, pro-Soviet President Khan proposed a new constitution that would formally install women's rights, but it was short-lived, and he was eventually killed. His replacement sought to separate from the previous alliance with the Soviet

Union. Meanwhile, the Islamist guerilla movement mujahadeen was gaining strength in the countryside with the intent to overthrow the government. In 1979 the Soviet Union invaded Afghanistan; the occupiers would remain for ten years. The mujahideen rebels would fight against the Soviets, and by 1987 the U.S. would quietly fund and arm them in an effort to overthrow communist rule in the war-torn country and prevent it from spreading. China and Britain provided similar aid, and the Soviets completely withdrew from Afghanistan in 1989.

In 1987, I knew nothing about any of this. I could barely have told you where Afghanistan was. The news in high school was about the Vietnam War, rock and roll, gas shortages, and the hostage crisis in Iran. In college, I focused less on current events than on school, ROTC, and work. Meanwhile, funding for the mujahideen was quietly approved by Congress. This strategic move was not widely known about by the war-weary public and remained hush-hush to a military that after Vietnam was rebuilding as an all-volunteer force.

When the Army sent me to Germany, I was focused on my new job, which primarily consisted of supporting the then-U.S. Customs Service mission by pre-clearing military flights, passengers, and cargo before they entered the United States.

One day at the Rhein-Main Air Base Field Office, I was instructed to clear a C-130 that was on the tarmac and not to ask any questions. That had my curiosity as I strode out to where it sat. When the ramp of the C-130 opened, I walked onto the aircraft. I was unprepared for what I experienced. The putrid smell of filth assaulted me as I gazed upon a handful of turban-bearing men who wore the look of a lifetime of war and hardship. These warriors had been secreted by the U.S. out of Afghanistan for treatment at a U.S. military hospital, after which they would be returned to the fight. We locked eyes, and I could not imagine their thoughts at seeing a uniformed Western woman upon landing. I remember wondering if I was the first one that they had seen after a lifetime of rugged existence and war in their home country. The significance of their purpose was lost on me, and I didn't know about the historical role they were playing in helping to stop the spread of communism. I signed the clearance papers and stepped off the aircraft. I had no idea that twenty years later, I would set foot in Afghanistan and view the ghosts of the Soviet occupation for myself.

In 1989, the Soviets withdrew from Afghanistan, and the mujahideen would split into warring factions competing for power without success. Into the void stepped the Taliban, an Islamic religious group that would at first bring some order and curb corruption but eventually imposed the strictest interpretation of Sharia law. This meant public executions of criminals and adulterers and amputations for those found guilty of theft. The Taliban trounced on any progress that Afghan women may have made towards basic civil liberties and restricted them to their homes if not with a male escort. They were not permitted to work or go to school and were forced to wear burkas that covered them from head to toe, with a small mesh screen to see out of into a haze. In "gender apartheid," women were essentially erased from public existence and were executed, tortured, or publicly whipped for what was determined to be the most minor infraction, such as skin that accidentally peeked out from under those stifling, indigo blue-colored garments.

The remnants of decades, even centuries of war in Afghanistan, were not only visible in the systemic oppression of women but in the abandonment of deadly detritus. Landmines from the Soviets and other occupiers peppered the landscape and took an incalculable toll on thousands of lives and limbs, many of them belonging to small children.

The people of Afghanistan were left holding the bag for removal of undetonated ordnance, dotting the terrain in almost every province. What the

Soviets discarded, the warring factions continued to add to in the years ensuing, and the problem of unexploded ordnance grew worse, not better. I read a recent report that over 41,000 Afghan soldiers and civilians have been killed by landmines since 1988.

There were no resources to clear out the jettisoned tanks and personnel carriers either. The hulking, rusting silhouette ghosts of wars past slept symbolically in the fields, in sharp contrast with the stunning snow-capped peaks of the majestic mountain ranges looming in the background.

I first witnessed the mujahideen on that aircraft in 1987 and symmetrically found myself in Afghanistan twenty years later in 2007. I was sent to review in-country training for National Guard and Army Reserve units after they mobilized to the Middle East. This was a time when the Global War on Terror was at its height, and funds flowed freely in support of troops, supplies, and equipment. Units would arrive at Ali Al Salem Air Base in Kuwait City, Kuwait. There, they would travel to U.S. facilities in Iraq, Afghanistan, and other places. Upon arrival to their destinations, they would receive valuable in-country training on counter-improvised explosive devices (IEDs), identification of enemy weapons and aircraft, Mine Resisted Ambush Protected (MRAP) vehicle rollover training, and much more. MRAPS were massive new vehicles that could withstand the explosions and heat of IED attacks and saved countless U.S. lives from insurgents. They had low centers of gravity and a unique hull shape but were prone to rollover accidents. By 2012 the short-lived, multi-billion-dollar MRAP program ended. It was eye-opening to witness these beasts, taller than a two-story building, and the training being conducted by our soldiers.

One day while outside, I became aware of people walking in a stooped manner in the distance, wearing what appeared to be some sort of very unsophisticated space suit. I asked about them and was told that these people were known as "bubble men." They were paid a small sum daily to go through fields and probe the ground, identifying undetonated landmines for marking. The individual explaining this to me said, "Yeah, every once in a while, one of them blows up." I was shocked. Could this be real? It appeared to be. It was heartbreaking to think that these people would put their life at risk every day for a small sum of money. I believed that stopping the spread of terrorism that had shaken our country to its very foundation and restoring some semblance of democracy to Afghanistan would result in a better life for these people, or so I hoped. Over the years, I developed an enduring fondness for the Afghan people that began when interacting with the base employees whom the U.S. hired to work in various positions on Bagram. Their lives had been pockmarked by war and tragedy, yet their fierce pride and resilience were evident in the broad smiles that erupted upon a warm greeting.

A few years after I left Bagram, I was a resident student at the U.S. Army War College. Our class was broken out into 20 small group seminars. Each seminar had two International Fellows from allied countries, and the Afghan Fellow was in my class. At noon during class, he would quietly exit to pray in the traditional manner of his devout Muslim faith. He was kind to everyone and added a tremendous perspective to our studies that year. Unlike almost all the other Fellows, he could not afford to bring his wife along. I learned not long ago that our friend and colleague was killed in the Taliban takeover and hasty U.S. withdrawal occurring in August, 2022. And the plight of girls and women? With all the gains made in improving their lives and education fresh in their recent memories, they once again had to resume their silent battle under the Taliban rule.

The systematic oppression of Afghan women continues on—the scars of endless wars leaving behind broken shells, broken equipment, broken tanks, broken people, and broken communities. The horror is eerily repeating itself in Ukraine as the Russians deliberately and relentlessly attack and destroy Ukrainian cities and people. The detritus of that invasion will remain and continue to inflict suffering long after the fighting somehow ends. After first witnessing the mujahideen warriors in 1987 and the ghosts of war in Afghanistan in 2007, I realized that the suffering of innocent lives at the hands of tyrannical rulers is an endless loop of a tragic tale.

Living in modern times doesn't change the fact that mistakes of the past are repeated in the present and the future. The ghosts of war return to haunt. Reflecting back provides perspective and understanding but can only prepare us and does not prevent tragedy.

When struggles persist,

find humor and cheer

on those who don't.

# 12

## *Cheer*

A Government Accounting Office report dated May 2020 indicated that while the percentage of women serving in the military had increased by one percent between 2004-2018, women were leaving at much higher rates than men. The reasons cited are aligned with some of the experiences I have described. That said, there has never been a better time for women to be in the Army than today. Almost all of the jobs are currently open to women, and the women volunteering for them are equal to the rigorous requirements—and equal to the men's. Strong role models are available now to guide and encourage them. Women are in more senior leadership roles than ever, demonstrating strength, grit, and grace. And best of all, those women are supporting, encouraging, and cheering on the ones coming in behind them.

For my generation, support networks were not readily available before we could communicate electronically. For the same reason, making friends at times was nearly impossible when the only female officer I had regular contact with was me, particularly in Germany. Germany had the most amazing beer that we could enjoy, monasteries and gorgeous castles to visit, endless festivals, and spice-scented Christmas markets where we could buy nutcrackers, decorated gingerbread hearts, and Polish pottery that adorn my own and so many others' kitchen shelves to this day. Germany also had my few living relatives who were thrilled to see me and who readily forgave my language errors. But Germany didn't have what I needed the most: another female my rank that I could bounce things off of.

When planning an operation in the Army, we use the terms "specified and implied tasks." It means that while the operations order states up front the objective or end-state, the details of how to get there must follow or no one will know how to execute. This is a metaphor for life for women who serve. We may know where we are going or where we want to go, but there are all kinds of decisions and unexpected barriers or obstacles we may not have considered along the way.

*Cycles.* Stress could throw our menstrual cycles off schedule, and we always had to be prepared. Sometimes this came with weight gain and excruciating pain, not great odds going into a physical fitness test. *Marriage.* Marriage to another service member is optimal but very hard to sustain with a family. Is our spouse going to follow our career or give up their own? Marriages outside of service involve sometimes painful decisions about who is going to give up what career-enhancing opportunity or give up completely. *Pregnancy.* If timed, forget about the time right before any known deployment or lengthy required schooling for professional development. Often as we all know, timing doesn't work. Additionally, many women choose to start their families midway or later in their careers. This comes with other issues sometimes. I didn't and was almost always the only junior officer I knew who was a young mother. Simultaneously mothering and soldiering was really difficult but incredibly rewarding at the same time. *Daycare.* If there is a family member who could do it, great! In my case, my husband traveled for his work after leaving the Army, and I would find myself praying at the end of each day that my boss didn't need anything else because the daycare was about to close.

Patrolling at night while in cadet and officer training was also fun when I was the only female in my squad. How I loved being out there breathing in the night air and absorbing all the sounds! We were issued night vision goggles to help us identify our training targets through the pitch-black landscape and communicated using standardized hand signals while walking silently. A raised fist meant "Stop." It was important to maintain what was called noise discipline. God forbid if someone sneezed. It was training, but the pressure was intense not to give away our position to the enemy (cadre), who would do us harm if they knew our location.

We had to stay hydrated and drink water. Eventually, this meant the need would arise to use the facilities—except that there were no facilities. How I resented my male counterparts, who could easily turn their backs and take care of business, not caring one way or the other if they were caught executing this simple biological task! For me, there were only choices. I could try to hold it forever. Or, I could hold up the entire squad by stating my intentions, which is not ideal. I could simply not tell anyone, quietly exit my place in the squad, hope my departure would not be detected, take care of business, and then rapidly but quietly catch up. I chose the latter. There was a (very) good chance I hadn't been missed. I was fast! However, the entire process was complicated by the sheer amount of equipment that needed to be unbuckled and let loose to the ground. A web belt containing an entrenching tool, ammunition cases, canteens, and more. Another belt dropped carrying my protective (gas) masks in the event of a (simulated) chemical attack. My rifle.

All placed on the ground, locations in the dark, all mentally recorded for ease of recovery. I couldn't step away too far, or I would certainly lose my squad. I would rapidly survey and analyze the shrubbery and quickly locate a promising tree or bush that possessed the requisite measurements. Then I would hastily work my way through the many steps of the female bio-break and squat behind it. As if the entire execution wasn't complex and stressful enough, my exposed butt cheeks could potentially glow like two ghostly orbs for anyone grabbing their night vision goggles at the precise moment. I could only hope my speed and stealth negated the likelihood of this occurrence!

Sometimes being female led to humorous and almost hilarious situations, more so upon reflection than execution. Once after a long day in basic training, we women returned to our barracks to find small rectangular boxes lined up at the foot of our tightly made-up bunks. Eyeing them suspiciously, we gingerly picked them up and opened them. A present? Well, kind of. Once opened, the packages revealed elongated sanitary napkins, thick as mini-mattresses, with strangely long tabs. My guess is that the tabs were supposed to be attached to some type of belt, which was not furnished and pre-dated more modern sanitary products. We all laughed when we saw them. They were so thick and impractical that none of us would have been able to wear them without walking with a waddle. It was ridiculous. After a lot of joking and laughing about these hefty and unusable, impractical pads, we turned them into boot rags and shined our boots with them. How comical to see us there, seated in the cool evenings on the barrack stoops as usual, carefully swiping sanitary napkins over the toes of our boots to bring them to the requisite glossy shine!

Whatever male had chosen them had no idea of what females actually needed. We appreciated the thought but not the follow-through. Though we were lighthearted about it, that didn't take away from the fact that these kinds of things were matters that males never even had to consider. For those of us lucky enough to have a manageable menstrual cycle, we just went about our business and tried to ignore the cramping. However, some females couldn't do that for reasons today that would be abundantly clear based on certain medical conditions. Some cycles would borderline take some females out. They would be bedbound by cramps or migraines to where they could hardly move. They would have to get a medical profile for this. Sadly, instead of being supportive, some of the females who pushed through would comment snarkily, "She's just weak." or "She's trying to make excuses to get out of training."

Then there was the hair issue. Males could shave their heads or get a close cut and be within regulation for at least a couple of weeks. Our hair couldn't touch the bottom of our collar, and that left us with a few options: very short hair or longer hair that could be arranged or put up in accordance with the (sometimes changing) regulations. Once, I cut my hair so short that my mother, who never weighed into those kinds of things, expressed her instant disapproval. Growing it out to where it was long enough to put up was the next challenge. I made it work between bands and a bunch of bobby pins that would inevitably fall out in training. Flyaway pieces of my hair would sneak out from under my helmet, presenting a sloppy and less-than-ideal image.

It didn't end with the hair. The standardized issue camouflage uniforms were made for men and were made straight up and down. There was a range of size options, but somehow were limited at the same time. For tops: Small, Short. Medium, Short. Medium, Long. Large, Medium. This went on. The pant sizes were also labeled similarly. Having fuller hips meant a larger size that needed cinching with the issued belt. Some women paid a tailor. Otherwise, there was this baggy look that was far less professional in appearance but not uncomfortable.

Once in training, we dug foxholes to the pleasant accompaniment of torrential rain. The faster I could displace dirt with my entrenching tool, the more the foxhole would fill with water. With rain making its way down into my uniform and soaking my underwear, I didn't think about complaining. "If it ain't raining, you ain't training!" Goes the old Army adage. My (male, of course) colleague broke with the— I'm certain— intellectual discussion we were having amidst this chaos. All of a sudden, he belted out a line from a Willie Nelson song…" Blue eyes CRYING, in the RAIN." Hahaha! I almost clocked him with the entrenching tool.

Sometimes being the only female meant working twice as hard only to receive an average rating. Advancing through the ranks meant praying I would come out on promotion lists. Being a mother for my entire career was not to my advantage because of needing to be in two places at once. Coming home from a hard day's work, my mind would race ahead: what to prepare for dinner, how to get two kids to different sports that were located many miles apart, and repeat the process as I picked them up. Reading to them at night, I hoped they didn't notice how stressed out I was. Planning their routine doctor's appointments on days that I knew nothing critical at work would happen and then praying that nothing critical at work happened. Showing up at PTA meetings in a new town to the chorus of, "Where are you from? Were you a cheerleader? What does your husband do? Wait you??? ARMY?" Sometimes I had to grit my teeth rather than answer with my trademark sarcastic wit. Over time, I felt fiercely proud of my choices and all that I had (sometimes barely) managed to accomplish.

I love being a woman veteran. As a group, we are growing but still a tiny percentage of the overall population. When I meet women veterans, we instantly share a mutual respect that is almost palpable. This cuts across all ranks. We, above all, understand the journey and how we got here. There is much debate on whether leaders are born or taught. I am more of the opinion that they are taught because everyone is a potential leader; it just looks different for each individual. We also learn from others' examples. In my mind, it is not just a privilege but a responsibility to reach out to other women who are not only serving but have served and offer support and anything else that our array of experiences and talent would suggest. The challenge of continuing to fight forward to make gains for our fellow females will always be there, and this is what each generation does.

Camaraderie builds swiftly
and lasts forever.

# 13

## *Camaraderie*

Previously, I wrote that leaving the Army was like being thrown off a speeding train. I repeat that here because the first thing I missed above all else was the camaraderie that began in basic training as we women arrived from all parts of the country, all socioeconomic backgrounds, all cultures, and all faiths. These designations were confiscated along with our civilian clothing as we donned our new uniforms and gradually became the soldiers we would be for life. Our shared experiences forged by proximity, sweat, sacrifice, and sometimes tears brought us together in a way that all veterans can understand. It is an unspoken bond with the strength of titanium, an undercurrent of meaning that is intangible and indescribable. It is an understanding that we have; we speak our own language; we have a profound and enduring respect for one another without having met; and we collectively feel the pain of losing our fellow servicemen and women. The term "benefits" often refers to housing allowance, medical care, or money for college, but the benefit of camaraderie is unspoken.

Sometimes being the only woman in the room, platoon, or staff resulted in feelings of isolation. I would find myself wondering if I was being treated differently, and if so, was it for being female? I vacillated between receiving better and worse treatment for the same activities as my male counterparts. Was it actual performance or reaction to my gender that drove actions towards me? I think many women can relate to the smallest example of somehow being stuck making the morning coffee when everyone drank it. In Zero Week of in-processing at Fort Benning, being the only junior enlisted female meant I spent that first week set aside, typing and filing in the airconditioned WWII buildings. My fellow male soldiers were out cutting the grass on the parade fields and picking up cigarette butts ("policing" the area). Those activities were not heavily supervised and allowed for some small talk; I longed to be a part of them. I longed for the outdoors in that fresh grass, inhaling its pungent scent. I longed to build those bonds that could not form while I was separated out for special treatment. The dogged and persistent feeling of going at it alone was my challenge to overcome. Female role models and trailblazers existed, but there were few, and there was no way to learn about most of them because we had no communications except for the newspaper and television. If I had pandered to these feelings, succumbing to loneliness would have been easy. Somewhere along the way, I learned the enduring skill of smiling through everything and of having a keen sense of humor. I wanted my peers to laugh because if they laughed, I could laugh, and I wanted so badly for them to include me. This helped tremendously in building connections, and humor became a part of my personal brand.

There was laughter in the simplest task (at the right time). In basic training, it was very hard not to snicker as drill sergeants barked out some commands. MOVE like you have a PURPOSE in your life! You are moving like POND WATER!! Get your HEAD out of your FOURTH POINT OF CONTACT!! We marched and ran to cadence calls that had not been sanitized for the benefit of females. Jody was both a nickname for the cadences and for the soldiers themselves. AIN'T NO USE IN GOING HOME...JODY'S GOT YOUR GIRL AND GONE! Always starting out on the left foot, the left foot hit the ground as the metronome of the cadences rang out.

We females could look around and make fun of ourselves in basic training. Those of us who were myopic were promptly issued square black glasses that much later would become stylish by Denzel

Washington. They had the common nicknames of "RPGs" which was an official acronym for Rocket Propelled Grenade, but to us meant Rape Prevention Glasses. The other term was BCGs for Birth Control Glasses. I laugh just to say it, and those terms endured as we received our issued glasses at annual eye exams throughout our careers. The price was certainly right if they broke! At one point in training, we lined up and had our headshots taken for our basic training "yearbook," our then-issued and now-phased out black poof (mushroom) hats perched sadly on our heads, the myopic half of us glumly staring at the camera through the black frames, unhappy about the memorializing of our pathetic appearance.

Next came the unfortunate haircuts and styles borne out of the Fort Dix "beauty shop." Army grooming standards have recently changed, but for many decades female hair could not touch the collar. In order to comply with the regulations, we placed our locks at the mercy of these "beauticians" who hastily chopped and fried our hair, leaving our appearance "cringeworthy" — a term that didn't yet exist. The goal was to roll out of our bunks in the morning, usually at 4:30, and conduct our personal hygiene as quickly as humanly possible. This meant a shower in which we barely had time to get wet, tooth brushing, running a comb through our hair, hastily dressing, and running to formation. Imagine having to braid, tie back, or pin-up hair—it could make us late, expended time, and often unraveled throughout the day. Females had to accept that we had that issue to deal with, and our male counterparts did not. So many of us meekly subjected ourselves to the shearing process. What the heck? It would grow back.

Food consumption in community settings is the universal language of camaraderie. Very early, I learned that the mess hall was a place where, while scarfing down our food in the brief time allotted, there was enough time to share our daily victories or burdens or even swap a few small stories about our hometowns and our families. Shoulder to shoulder, we talked and laughed and shared. There was food bargaining: if you give me your dessert, you can have my roll. Minutes went by quickly, and we received the sign. Our chairs scraped the floors, and everything was assembled back on the trays, which were emptied and stacked as our paces quickened and we donned our covers (caps). To exit a building without your military-issued cover squared on your head was always a forbidden practice, violations of which were rewarded with many, many pushups. Our brief respite was over; the next one would come up as quickly as the pace by which we conducted our breathtaking training.

It was not just the mess halls that gave us a pause to bond over food. While out training, we consumed rations whose names, contents, and packaging have continued to evolve with the passage of time. I entered the Army early enough to enjoy the rations left over from the Vietnam War era, packaged in little olive drab-colored tins and known as C-Rations. These came with a small tool known as a P-38 which was a manual can opener. It had a little hole and could be attached to a small cord for safekeeping. Knowing what a P-38 is can give away a veteran's age bracket.

Mixed together, we gleefully created concoctions. For example, we would moisten our freeze-dried strawberries and add dried coffee creamer. The delectable porridge was then drizzled over our dried shortbread—the best recipe for dessert ever! We had no choice, of course, as to what would arrive in those boxes of cans, and eagerly awaited the good stuff (spaghetti and tomato sauce or little hot dogs) while watching the faces fall of the hapless souls who would draw the short straw (Spam-like meat). The bartering and trading would begin rapidly; barter too long, and we didn't eat. These food swaps created some laughter and strengthened the bonds that were in continuous motion. Although someone was always disappointed in their swap, there was always the next meal.

Shared community over food pleasantly persisted throughout the passage of time and our careers. Operations Enduring Freedom and Iraqi Freedom deployed soldiers overseas for over 20 years. Over time, mess halls in Kuwait, Afghanistan, and Iraq brought in award-winning chefs to boost morale for troops fortunate enough to have access to them. The holidays saw ice sculptures and even an exquisite ice swan who held butter pats in the curve of her gracefully carved back. Our dessert selections were worthy of 5-star ratings. We had salad buffets and ice cream bars. It is no secret that mess hall food choices can be very high calorie for the most part, so if we were not in constant motion or had no time for a fitness routine, we had to be very, very careful about what ended up on our trays.

Shared experiences create powerful bonds. On difficult missions, in working for tough bosses, in grueling training, and even in sad moments, we veterans have the skill of instantly recognizing someone that we shared an experience with twenty, thirty years later, and beyond. We moved constantly and worked with teammates over the course of a career, lost touch and yet those bonds never went away. This same concept applies to all of the family members we meet along the way. Over the years, I have seen my brothers and sisters in arms lose each other, spouses, parents, and children; and loss is a great equalizer that causes us to wrap our physical and virtual arms around each other.

At one time, I worked in a three-star general officer-level Army directorate in the Pentagon. An annual social event was something that we all thoroughly enjoyed and looked forward to—usually a picnic that involved activities for the kids and sports events. Due to our advancing age, someone always came away from those sporting events on crutches. As the social coordinator that year, I polled the office with some suggestions, and we all agreed to hold a 60s and 70s-themed bowling night at the Fort Belvoir, Virginia bowling alley. It was all there: a dazzling disco ball to set the tone for our theme, six dedicated bowling lanes, and a place to enjoy our pizza and sodas. The management team gladly accommodated our requests for themed music. We could not stop laughing as senior officers and non-commissioned officers arrived to the Bee-Gees' music, dressed in Afro wigs, long sideburns, leisure suits of fine polyester (one was powder blue), and hippy gear such as fringed leather jackets, tie-dyed T-shirts, go-go boots and wigs with long hair and no bangs parted in the middle. Some found these gems in their aging parents' closets, and others found them in thrift shops. The hilarious aspect of the costumes and bowling juxtaposed the serious nature of our work that evening and created memories that last to this day.

When I took my first oath in January of 1983, I signed up to join the Army for the same reasons that so many of us did: travel, adventure, escape, college money, and job security. The future was a vast unknown. Things got very rough sometimes, but the camaraderie made the struggles, the barriers, and the obstacles fade from my memory. Today, I play it forward by volunteering to provide support not just to veterans but to young adults who are thinking about the military as a career. They energize me. I have to admit my soft spot for the women. We have, in the recent words of a female four-star general, come a long way, but there is still a long way to go. We must give it our best each day, and be there for each other.

www.ingramcontent.com/pod-product-compliance
Lightning Source LLC
Chambersburg PA
CBHW032230080426
42735CB00008B/796